AMARNA & THE BIBLICAL EXODUS
Gods in Ruins

Dirk Schroeder

CAMBRIDGE PARCHMENTS

Did the Exodus really happen?

Did Pharoah die in the Red Sea, as the Bible says??

Were the Hebrews really given most of Egypt's gold?

Did the Egyptian army actually perish all together?

Has Pharoah's dead firstborn ever been found?

... the documentary and archaeological evidence discussed in this book gives a resounding YES to all these questions as well as revealing WHY it happened and adding incontrovertible external proof of Scripture, with dozens of additional points of proof also.

The Exodus is the only credible explanation for the Amarna period that followed.

Akhenaten was not a pacifist... he just had a missing army!

md.schroeder2015@gmail.com

ISBN-13: 978-1999618377   BIC: HDDG & HRKP1

FIRST EDITION

published by
CAMBRIDGE PARCHMENTS

Introduction

Only a monumental catastrophic event such as the Biblical Exodus, with the 10 Plagues that preceded it—treated as a historical event by Josephus, Manetho, Syncellus, Lysimachus, Chaeremon, Herodotus, the Hebrew Scriptures and the early Christian writings—could have discredited the many Egyptian gods so suddenly and convincingly, and laid the basis for their replacement with just one seemingly powerful god, as Akhenaten* did, creating his reputation as a 'pacifist', 'heretic' and even an 'atheist'! —more about that later!

That event is surely the only credible explanation for the desperate and momentous situations that the Canaanite 'Amarna[1] Letter' writers reveal in their passionate pleas for military support and continued life, as well as gold supplies, in at least 170 of those amazing discovered letters.

The Hebrew *Bible** says that Egypt's world-beating army was totally wiped out by drowning in the Red Sea; that the great Pharoah himself also drowned there; that the escaping enslaved Hebrews (Israelites*) actually 'stripped the Egyptians' of their gold and silver when the Egyptian people voluntarily showered them with massive amounts of it. Also that the firstborn son of the Pharoah (we use this expression interchangeably* with 'king') was killed in the 10th plague, resulting in a sibling taking over the throne thereafter (names are not given in the *Bible*).

The startling facts, context and harrowing subjective perspectives revealed in the Amarna Letters can surely only be explained by the sequence of events outlined in considerable detail in the book of Exodus in Hebrew Scripture (we use this expression interchangeably* with '*Bible*', '*Torah*' and 'Hebrew *Bible*').

Many more facts are discussed here in a new light in this fascinating and very important study.

*see the Appendix for a list of interchangeable spellings, titles and words used throughout the book

Footnotes and References are listed at back of the book, along with picture attributions.

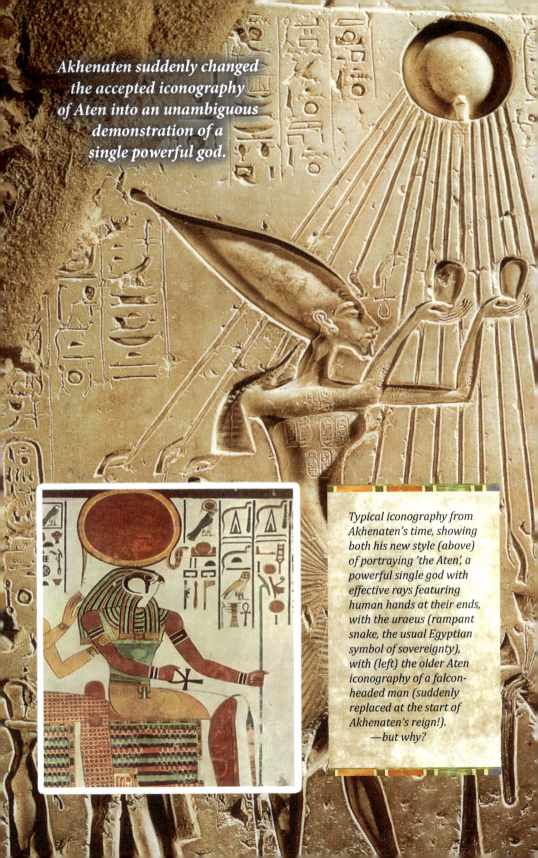

Akhenaten suddenly changed the accepted iconography of Aten into an unambiguous demonstration of a single powerful god.

Typical iconography from Akhenaten's time, showing both his new style (above) of portraying 'the Aten', a powerful single god with effective rays featuring human hands at their ends, with the uraeus (rampant snake, the usual Egyptian symbol of sovereignty), with (left) the older Aten iconography of a falcon-headed man (suddenly replaced at the start of Akhenaten's reign!).
—but why?

Amazingly, the body of the young firstborn son of Pharoah has been found and identified! —the culmination of the 10 plagues.

The well-preserved mummy proven to be of Crown Prince Djhutmose 'B', the firstborn son of Amenhotep III, and who evidently died from unknown causes at around age 11. This mummy has been found in the same tomb as Amenhotep III and Queen Tiye, and with other linking evidence described in Chapter 4 of this book.

Hundreds of cuneiform 'Amarna Letters' testify to the lack of an Egyptian army (in fact Akhenaten is famously now popularly dubbed a 'pacifist'), and also the letters speak much about a major lack of gold, in addition to reference to the tragic loss of the previous Pharoah, evidently Amenhotep III.

This matches the amazing account found in the Hebrew Bible (and Torah) chapter of 'Exodus'; see Chapter 3 of this book.

Most of the hundreds of ancient Amarna Letters speak of the missing Egyptian army, as well as the almost total lack of gold

... just as the Bible describes the Exodus!

—read the translations in this book!

Akhenaten suddenly changed his own name from a reference to the god Amun to the public recognition of 'the Aten'; also demanding that other people changed their names

Amen-Hotep IV changed his name to Akhen-Aten in recognition of the discrediting of the thousands of Egyptian gods (including Amun) , whose images he systematically destroyed along with their temples and support systems. Also highly significant is the fact that he was the second-born son of Amenhotep III; his elder brother Crown Prince Djhutmose died young of unknown cause.

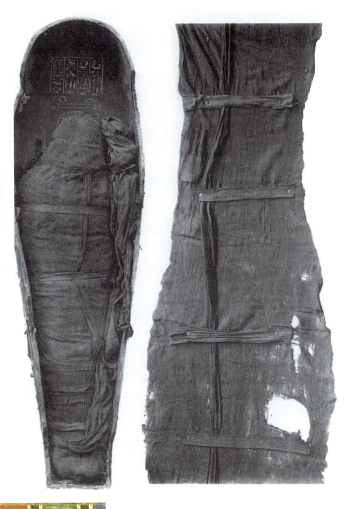

Amenhotep III coffin and shroud, showing the relatively humble and rough treatment he received after his death.

His tomb and also many statues of him appear to have been treated with very significant contempt after his death; many statues of him were later re-modelled to represent Rameses II.

Was Amenhotep III the Pharoah that lost his entire army?

Amenhotep III, very likely the Pharoah of the Exodus; his body is mutilated and embalmed in a strangely unique manner.

Why this book?

Have you ever had a *"Eureka! Eureka!"* moment?

Mine came when I realised more deeply the content of most of the *Amarna Letters*; the highly distinctive situation they described, relating to missing Egyptian gold, a consistently missing Egyptian army, a tragic Pharoah death, and a second-born Egyptian king taking the place of a suddenly missing first-born! That sounds uniquely like Exodus chapter 12 to me, from the Hebrew *Bible* (including its *Torah,* the first five books).

A typical Amarna Letter of which 382 have been found, to date.

Unlike Archimedes, I have not run shouting excitedly through the streets with that famous double exclamation, but have decided to put together the above points, and many others found in continued research into sources relating to the Exodus, Amarna, and 'the Aten'. The *Egypt Exploration Society* director Chris Naunton said recently that there are not many truly exciting moments of discovery these days, but indeed what a thrill it is when one is made!

There have been many very popular books propounding theories about Akhenaten (or Amen-Hotep IV as he was named initially, as king, in deference to the god Amun [Amen]) but they all miss the really major evidence relating to the historical Exodus and its preceding '10 plagues'. This book is not intended or claimed to be an exegesis of Scripture, but a proposed explanation that widely and convincingly fits both Scripture and what is known or generally accepted currently about the Amarna period, other than the traditionally accepted dating for the Exodus (but which is increasingly disputed by many scholars).

I only consider myself to be a part-time, now retired, 'egyptologist' despite my extensive travels and interest in the topic, and my diploma degree does nothing to qualify me for this. However, I wouldn't be the first 'outsider' to objectively see what looks plain from a different vantage point.

It is clear that something very, very powerful must have made Akhenaten change his nation's worship to just one god. Most writers have glossed over this motivation, in my opinion, with inadequate reasoning on the conflicting power of priests, switching the income stream, etc.

For the first time, this is a book that *fully* supports the Hebrew *Bible* (along with matching detail in the *Qur'an*) and gathers the current learning into a work that proves, beyond reasonable doubt, by a fresh assessment of several hundred items of circumstantial, written and tomb-based items of evidence that the Exodus and the '10 plagues' actually happened, as the Hebrew *Bible* describes, and as mirrored in the *Qur'an* and *Josephus.*

Yves Bonnefoy, in his great work *Mythologies*, Vol.1 p184, says:

> *"[The Bible] constitutes a mine of information about all aspects of the West Semitic religions, including those foreign to the religion of Israel. This mine has still been exploited only sporadically and somewhat tendentiously, that is to say solely or almost solely from a biased point of view and within the context of an implacable struggle between the*

religion of revelation, namely that of Israel, and the 'barbarian' practices of the other Western Semites., called 'Canaanites' ."

Why ignore such a unique and valuable 'mine'? 'Bias' can pertain not only to different religious views but also to great unfounded scepticism and also ignorance, deliberate or otherwise.

Encyclopaedia Britannica says, *"behind legends is a solid core of fact"* - and all scholars would likely agree with that.

In all the books ever published about Amarna, we've had the historical, archaeological or artistic findings expounded quite extensively— but what about the religious aspect? This has been something of a black hole. Like it or not, the best source for early explanations regarding these aspects is the Hebrew *Bible*, probably compiled initially in the 2nd millennium BCE from other ancient sources then available; these are used in sections starting variously at Genesis 1:1, 2:4, 5:1, 6:9, 10:1, 11:10, 11:27, 25:12, 36:1 and 37:2 – also 2 Kings 1:18 and other similar references to earlier primitive writings or 'books'. Moses was highly fluent in both Egyptian and Hebrew languages, and maybe others, being trained as a prince in Egypt and being a natural Israelite of the scholarly and priestly tribe of Levi.

Maybe like me, you find it hard to accept the thin reasonings often presented in articles and books regarding Akhenaten's 'revolution', excellent though the actual research usually is at a secular level. It surely had to be something exceedingly powerful, and very convincing at the time, to the priests and the people alike, though somewhat temporary (lasting only 16 years at most) and causing no recorded public spiritual rebellion. Let's see what that motivation was, with preserved or discovered evidence from the most authentic writings made at or near the time by a prominent highly literate princely Egyptian Hebrew, as well as many other regional leaders of the time, in inscriptions and the Amarna letters, as well as the sacred books.

Weak objections answered

Commonly-accepted Egyptian chronology (but which is now seriously being questioned), argues against the proposition in this book. However, the circumstantial evidence very strongly indicates that Amenhotep III was the 'Exodus Pharoah' and that his second-born son Akhenaten was the subsequent king who created the 'Amarna period' as a result. Many archaeologists and related professionals from many disciplines are now building convincing evidence of this link.

Also, the 'co-regency' theory relating to Amenhotep III and IV seems at first to make the Amarna and Exodus link impossible. However, the only seemingly credible 'evidence' for a co-regency relates to the 'Huy' tomb at Luxor, and the official report[2] on it lacks any proof for the dating of the inscriptions. All it proves is that 'Huy' worked during the reigns of both kings. Other refutation is also discussed in Chapter 4 of the book.

AMARNA MYSTERIES NOW SOLVED:

Pharoah Akhenaten, who made huge changes to the culture and religion of Egypt in the 18th Dynasty.

1. *Did the Exodus really happen?*

2. *Who was the Exodus Pharoah?*

3. *Why was no army sent to support the Canaan vassals?*

4. *Why was virtually no gold sent to Canaan?*

5. *Why was Akhenaten a second-born Pharoah?*

6. *How did Amenhotep III die?*

7. *How were thousands of gods discredited, at a stroke?*

8. *Why was 'the Aten' depicted as rays of the sun, with no name?*

9. *Where is the body of Pharoah's dead firstborn son?*

10. *Who influenced Akhenaten in his monotheism?*

11. *Why did Akhenaten's Amarna 'plan' not succeed?*

12. *Why no dialogue between Amenhotep III & Akhenaten?*

Match the Bible account with actual history...

1. Total loss of Egypt's army	12 points of evidence*
2. Loss of most Egypt gold	14 points, incl 12 Letters[2]
3. Tragic death of older Pharoah	13 points of evidence
4. Sudden mysterious death of firstborn	3 points of evidence
5. Sudden leaving of all Hebrews	1 point of evidence
6. Public discrediting of old Egypt gods	2 points of evidence
7. Shamed memory of older Pharoah	3 points of evidence
8. Recognition of a sole uniquely powerful god	13 points of evidence
9. New Pharoah would be second-born	1 point of evidence
10. New Pharoah's mother likely in charge	2 points of evidence

including almost all of the 382 Amarna Letters.

Contents : and an overview

Chapter 8: THE 'HAPIRU' : WERE THEY THE HEBREWS?

A discussion of the evidence, with scepticism about a link with the Hebrews.

Appendix:

'Stroll in the garden' at the new city of Amarna

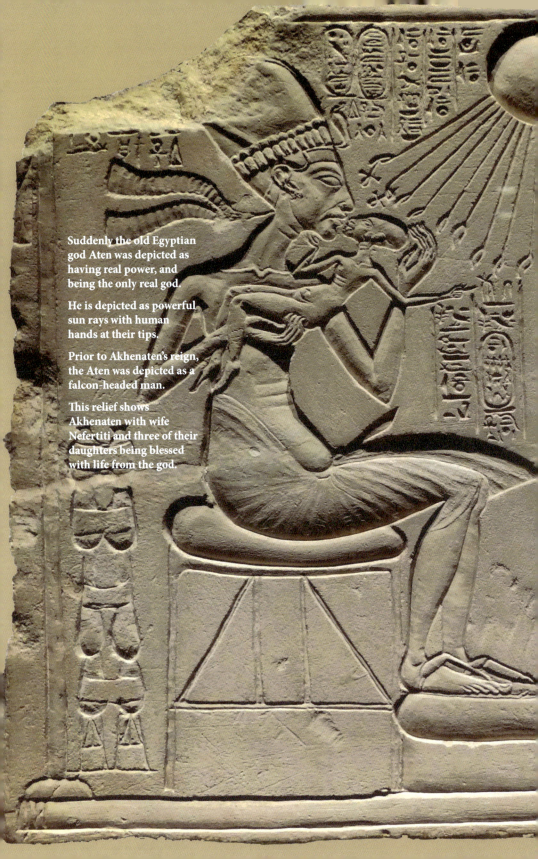

Suddenly the old Egyptian god Aten was depicted as having real power, and being the only real god.

He is depicted as powerful sun rays with human hands at their tips.

Prior to Akhenaten's reign, the Aten was depicted as a falcon-headed man.

This relief shows Akhenaten with wife Nefertiti and three of their daughters being blessed with life from the god.

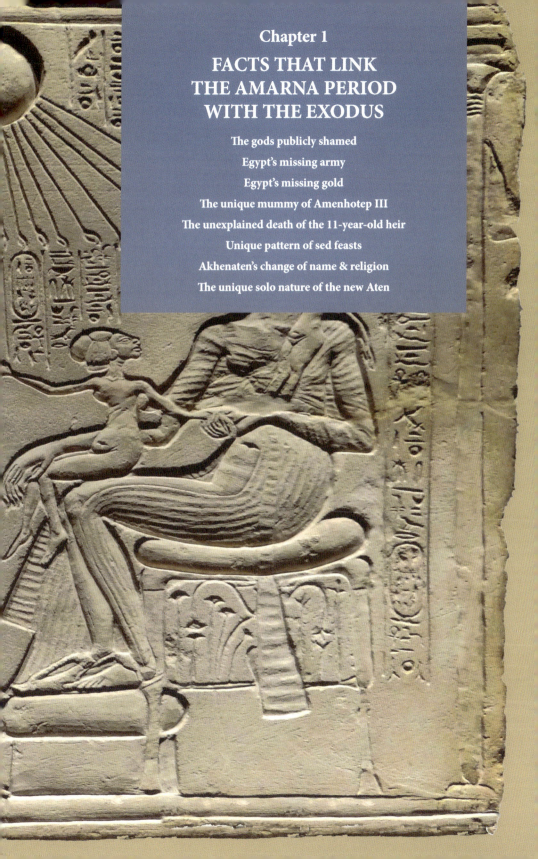

Chapter 1

FACTS THAT LINK
THE AMARNA PERIOD
WITH THE EXODUS

The gods publicly shamed

Egypt's missing army

Egypt's missing gold

The unique mummy of Amenhotep III

The unexplained death of the 11-year-old heir

Unique pattern of sed feasts

Akhenaten's change of name & religion

The unique solo nature of the new Aten

Major evidence for the Exodus and an Amarna link:

The old gods were all discredited and publicly shamed at the same time.

The Egyptian army is uniquely missing during this period.

Horses are depicted only in a ceremonial, not military, role.

Soldiers are only depicted in ceremonial roles, or as foreign mercenaries.

Akhenaten, even if he trained a new army, seems fearful of fighting the Hebrews.

Egyptian gold is uniquely lacking during this period, just as Exodus explains.

A new emphasis on 'Truth' contrasts with the 'false' and dark religions and gods.

The huge religious change was unchallenged as a 'heresy' at the time.

The Aten now featured as the sole nameless truly powerful god rather than as an idol.

The Aten featured 'hands' at the end of each ray, reflecting recent divine experience.

Aten's change from falcon-headed to power-disk matches the timing of the Exodus.

'God' terminology suddenly destroys the need for a category of 'gods' ('neter').

Amenhotep III died suddenly, tragically, inexplicably, referred to as 'tragic death'.

Amenhotep III's mummy shows a violent death, being torn apart.

Amenhotep III's mummy was embalmed in a unique way with much resin.

Amenhotep III's mummy contains bird skeletons.

Amenhotep III's tomb is strangely unfinished and lacking proper status.

Amenhotep III's tomb contained a 'hub of a fine chariot'; likely related to his death.

Amenhotep III was a great builder, just as the Bible indicates.

Amenhotep III held strangely-timed frequent 'sed' feasts to raise the spirits of the people.

The Bible describes the Plagues, Pharoahs and Exodus in a way that matches this period.

Akhenaten was the second-born heir as Pharoah.

Akhenaten held a uniquely early 'sed' feast to raise the spirits of his bewildered people.

Amarna period 'was a reaction, not a planned revolution'; reaction to what?

Tiye wears royal crown demonstrating a temporary 'de facto' sole-ruler status.

Tiye addressed as though de-facto Queen while 2nd-born son still too young to rule.

Crown Prince Djhutmose died as firstborn heir, at a young age.

Crown Prince Djhutmose cause of death not evident.

Crown Prince Djhutmose buried with Tiye and same tomb as Amenhotep III.

Evidence for a co-regency between Amenhotep III and Akhenaten is lacking.

Ancient historians credit this period with the link to the Exodus.

Moses and other contemporary Hebrews were very likely to have influenced Akhenaten.

Other viziers and royal personnel are thought to have been Semitic.

AKHENATEN (AMENHOTEP IV) is popularly noted for his sudden enforcing of the whole population of Egypt to turn to monotheism, quite suddenly discarding the apparently hundreds of discredited gods of Egypt which they had revered for centuries.

Why did he do this? What cataclysmic momentous and mind-numbing event allowed him to present this as the way forward, unchallenged?

Akhenaten is widely noted for his apparent 'pacifism'... but could it be that he actually had no army for most of his reign? Was it actually destroyed in the Red Sea, as the Hebrew *Bible* says? Just think of the consequences.

The 'Amarna letters' include complaints (EA 26 & 27) from a Canaanite king that a gold statue had not arrived as promised from the royals of Egypt, and that the substitute statue lacked the lavish (solid!) gold that was expected... was this because, as the Hebrew *Bible* says in Ex 12:36, the Egyptians gave much of their gold to the Hebrews, "*stripping them*" as they left Egypt in miraculous glory? Prior to that, gold was said to be as plentiful "*as dust in the land of my brother*". Many other letters repeat unprecedented demands for reinstating the massive supplies of gold that were promised, or regularly expected, but which had evidently ceased, with no explanation given.

Akhenaten succeeded[1] Amenhotep III as Pharoah, yet he was not the firstborn son. His elder brother, the firstborn 'Crown Prince Thutmose [Djhutmose]' evidently died young, probably aged about 11, without becoming a ruler. Didn't the Hebrew *Bible* say that all the firstborn in Egypt died in an act of God, in the 10th plague? It is possible with the right permissions to actually see his intact mummy, even now in the 21st century!

Debates about a co-regency of Amenhoteps III and IV still rage, despite a confident but questioned proclamation by Mohamed Ibrahim Ali, head of the *Egyptian Antiquities Ministry,* in 2014[4] that 'conclusive' evidence for a co-regency had been found in a 1978 dig. Doubt exists though because the 'Amen-Hotep-Huy' tomb column inscriptions they boldly dated to the 30th year of Amenhotep III still apparently have no evidence for that dating, and the tomb's occupant may have been alive well beyond year 35... for he is known to have been supervising the Gebel El Silsila quarry works through much of both reigns. The fact that the tomb features cartouches of both Amenhotep III and IV simply shows surely that Huy worked under both kings, not necessarily at the same time. This is discussed in more detail in Chapter 4.

Akhenaten featured not the actual Sun in his new monotheistic worship, but the powerful light from the sun... the rays shown with hands on the end of each, as if recognising the Creator who could literally be 'hands-on', really making powerful events happen, and should be the One they now recognised as superior to all their gods now so discredited, specifically in the 10 plagues, and the subsequent Exodus, showing them to be no-gods, all now in ruins.

There follows here a presentation of around 35 main facts (including the ones discussed later in the book), some recently discovered, to show how the Hebrew *Bible* makes the best sense of one of the most puzzling episodes in

Wadjet, the useless cobra-headed goddess, one of the previously popular gods of Egypt and supposed protector of the Pharoah and all Egypt; he was the basis of the uraeus motif which represents sovereignty.

history. These are discussed in more detail, with additional points and references, in later chapters.

A 2016 reconsideration of the ancient Egyptian mummies from the 18th Dynasty was conducted by the *American Association of Physical Anthropologists* and published in their *Journal*[5]. Previous identifications of mummies relevant to our period of interest (Amenhotep III and Queen Tiye) were confirmed, with re-assessment of 'ancient DNA profiling' and CT scanning, using radiology, blood and hair identification, and molecular genetics.

■ THE INEFFECTIVE EGYPTIAN GODS & IDOLS WERE COMPLETELY AND PUBLICLY SHAMED, APPARENTLY QUITE SUDDENLY

An astounding change took place at the start of Akhenaten's reign as king. From the long-held esteem for and worship of up to 2,000 gods, demi-gods and demons the Egyptians changed to recognising only one, more powerful, god. How could any leader justify such a monumental change? Why would the public accept it at all?

There seems to have been no rebellion, neither by priests nor the public; no explicit theological refutation or discussion; no accusation of 'heresy' at the time. What catastrophic failure was there of the thousand gods?

Only the monumental publicly-seen failure of the old gods could have provided the political and ideological platform for such a comprehensive and historic change. Chapters 3 through 5 will look at this.

■ FALSENESS OF THE PREVIOUS RELIGIOUS ORDER EXPOSED

Akhenaten, though quite young, must have been deeply affected by the falseness and ineffectiveness of the old gods, and maybe the corruption and abuse by their priests, which was specifically referred to comprehensively in one of his early lengthy inscriptions at Amarna, a huge boundary stone at the northern extremity of Amarna:

> *"my oath of Truth, which is my desire to pronounce, and of which I will not say 'It is false' eternally forever.... For, as Father (Hor-Aten) liveth... priests, more evil are they than those things which I have heard unto year 4, more evil are they than those things which I have heard in the year... more evil are they than...   that the king ... heard, more evil are they than which Menkheperura heard... in the mouth of negroes, in the mouth of any people."*

Going much further than public declarations of the ineffectiveness of the old gods, Akhenaten set about actually destroying almost all vestiges of them; the inscriptions, the names, the temples, the priestly employment, the support system, ... even the plural word 'gods' was wiped away permanently! Very few gods or idols escaped this action. Chapters 4 through 6 discuss more detail.

Akhenaten even changed his earlier name (Amen-Hotep) in disgust at Amun ('Amen'). Also his first child, and some others subsequently, were named with the newly respected Aten embedded in their names.

■ THE BIBLE HAS ALWAYS BEEN CORRECT

The many aspects of evidence relating to the Amarna period seem to me to shout out that the Exodus and the Plagues must have immediately preceded this period. Very few others have seen this link; most have invented some wild 'fringe' theories which at best have only scant suggestion of a fit with the facts.

The difference seems to be the relative trust, or distrust, of the accuracy of the Hebrew *Bible* account, and a holding firmly to the strength of traditional Egyptological chronologies which would seem, on the surface, to make the fit unlikely. See Chapter 7, and the Appendix.

Maybe we should learn from many previous scepticisms where ultimately the sacred Scriptures have always been proven to be correct. For example, some 'experts' mocked the Hebrew *Bible's* 50 or more references to the Hittites for many years, yet ultimately that tribe became one of the best attested tribes of all ancient peoples. The 1906 excavation by Hugo Winckler and Theodor Makridi at Boghazhoi (Anatolia) revealed 30,000 tablet fragments from the Hittite royal archives in addition to an entire city and nation of ancient civilisation. Yet before that period of rediscovery in the 19th century, there seemed to be no external or archaeological evidence for their existence. Some cited the missing evidence as proof that the *Bible* was fabricated myth.

The same also for other ancient 'Genesis' places such as Ur, Babel, Sheba and many others... doubted at one time, but supported externally later.

The highly regarded archaeologist W. F. Albright said[6],

> " 'The Table of Nations' (Genesis chapter 10) remains an astonishingly accurate document".

Henry Rawlinson concurred when he wrote[7] that Genesis well deserves...

> "... to be called the most authentic record that we possess for the affiliation of nations."

The Hebrew *Bible* does refer to Waset, at Nahum 3:8 and Ezekiel 30:16 where the old Hebrew equivalent name 'No-Amon' is used, and an abbreviated 'No'. (Heliopolis is called 'On').,

The lack of specific reference to the Exodus within Egypt's own textual and archaeological history is not surprising; as they say, "*lack of evidence is not evidence of lack*"! The ancient Egyptian kings had to be 'good gods' as well as good leaders, thus it was necessary for them to seen as conquerors, not the vanquished! The records we do have emphasise the supremacy of the king over his enemies, and reference to the festivals and offerings relating to this.

■ EGYPT'S MISSING ARMY

Akhenaten is noted for his apparent 'pacifism'... yet it could be that he actually had no army! Was the lost Egyptian army replaced? What evidence is there that Akhenaten fought virtually no wars? Around 170 of the 382 'Amarna let-ters' from the minor vassals and kings of Canaan speak of the virtually total lack of Egyptian troops which had always previously, under Amenhotep III, been ready, willing and able to defend them there in Canaan. There is only a scant military presence mentioned in any letter, and mostly the army is miss-ing completely, giving rise to truly desperate pleas. See Chapter 2.

Akhenaten seems indifferent to any relationship with the Canaanite Tush-ratta, beyond the Red Sea. His letters, which seem to be relatively few, at best give – empty – promises for 'archers' or commissioners to be sent into Ca-naan; none of these is recorded as having been fulfilled. Mostly his letters ask the Canaanite kings to guard themselves!

■ AMARNA RELIEFS SHOW SOLDIERS ONLY IN CEREMONIAL ROLE

The 'soldiers' relief from Amarna (*Fitzwilliam Museum, Cambridge, UK*) shows two soldiers, probably Nubian (note the wigs) and armed only with clubs, being prepped for a royal parade (looking quite untrained, one of them holding his shield very amateurishly, true to life at the time, most likely!) This is typical of reliefs of the period when soldiers or weapons are depicted.

Another example is the depiction of weapons and shields at the site of the 'window of appearance' at Amarna, but these are static displays of potential military or civil defence resources, rather than active military items. (*Museum of Fine Arts, Boston; 63.427*)

Several of these Amarna reliefs (some of them in the discreet *Brooklyn Museum of Art*; another there in the magnificent *Israel Museum (see picture on opposite page)* in Jerusalem depict ceremonial equestrian activity, not military; the horses' manes are prepared decora-tively for ceremony, not battle; they have long tails which look grander for public

Relief displayed in the Fitzwilliam Museum, Cambridge UK, depicting some soldiers being prepared for a royal parade.

duty; the rider is seen carrying sandals (for him to walk alongside the chariot for part of the journey, possibly in a commute between palace and temple); the harness and the horse head pose is clearly ceremonial; these chariots and horses are invariably shown in these commute, parade, or cavalcade situa-tions. None is a commemoration of military victory or skirmish of that period.

■ LIBYAN MERCENARIES FEATURED AS THE ONLY ACTIVE SOLDIERS

Artefacts such as the fine *British Museum* papyrus fragments EA74100 show mercenaries from Libya and Mycenae, who were possibly drafted in during that Amarna period as an internal police or civil defence force; their 'enemies' appear to be individual Egyptians. Chapter 2 has more detail.

■ WAS THERE AN EFFECTIVE REPLACEMENT ARMY?

The 'restoration inscription' of King Tutankhamun, from his reign soon after the Amarna period declares that he *"repaired what was ruined... and repelled the disorder throughout the two lands"* and significantly it continues, *"IF an army was sent to Djahy, no success came from it."*

■ AKHENATEN SEEMS FEARFUL OF MILITARY ACTION IN CANAAN

One can imagine that following a humiliating and totally crushing defeat at the Red Sea, the new king (Akhenaten) would be extremely reluctant to send a fresh newly-recruited army (even if he had one) to chase after the departing Hebrews, now that they and their almighty super-naturally backed hordes were known to be in Canaan, Sinai or Paran somewhere. 'Once bitten, twice shy', as they say. Even if the Hebrews were just aimlessly wandering around the Sinai and Southern Canaanite desert, they would be deemed to be a potential death-dealing force following their recent escape through the Red Sea. The Hebrew *Bible* does refer to many of these wandering Hebrews as 'men of war' in that period; Deuteronomy 2:14 says[8],

Relief displayed in the Israel Museum, Jerusalem, depicting what is acknowledged as Ceremonial horses with a royal chariot.

> *"The time that we spent walking from Kadesh-Barnea until we crossed the Wadi Zered was 38 years, until that whole generation of warriors had perished from the camp".*

Relief displayed in the tomb of Merye, showing the usual Ceremonial horses with royal chariots under the blessing of the Aten.

Amenhotep III;
huge statue in
British Museum.

Some think that these 'men of war' were the 'Apiru' (Hapiru/ Habiru) referred to so frequently in that period... but see Chapter 8 of this book.

3. SILENCE OF RELATIONS BETWEEN AMENHOTEP III AND AKHENATEN

The fact that there is a total lack of recorded correspondence, or other inter-action, between Amenhotep III and his son and successor Akhenaten (Amen-hotep IV), indicates strongly that Amenhotep III died unexpectedly.

Chapter 4 deals with the co-regency idea.

■ AMENHOTEP III DIED SUDDENLY, TRAGICALLY

An Amarna letter (EA26) from Tushratta shows that Akhenaten is nominally ruling at the time of condolence for the loss of Amenhotep III, with widow Tiye being in charge with some authority or influence over the young son, known as Amenhotep IV. There appears to be no co-regency with his father. Chapter 4 of this book will look at this in more detail.

Amarna letter EA29, written to Akhenaten about death of the king (obviously the previous king) being tragic when he *"went to"* his ('fate') death;

> *"When my brother, [Amenhotep III], went to his fate it was reported. When I heard what was reported... I grieved, saying, "Let even me be dead, or let 10,000 be dead in my country, and in my brother's country 10,000 as well, but let my brother, whom I love and who loves me, be alive as long as heaven and earth."*

We have a letter, therefore, that gives us some context about the death of Amenhotep III which, if he indeed was the Pharaoh of the Exodus could be consistent with his death in the Red Sea, or at least not contradictory. He thus literally 'went to' his tragic death or 'fate'.

Amenhotep III's wife Tiye evidently took over rulership[1] for a while at end of his reign, and received at least one of the Amarna letters (EA26) on a king's behalf; as you'd expect, if the king died suddenly, and his first son was killed, exactly as outlined in the book of Exodus; a young second-born son would take some time to prepare or be old enough to take responsibility as the new king. This was Akhenaten, quite unprepared for royal leadership[1].

■ AMENHOTEP III MUMMY INDICATES TRAGIC WATERY DEATH

A unique embalming process with a type of resin was used for the mummy of Amenhotep III: the embalmers had unusually packed the skin of the deceased king with a new resinous material, and the body seems 'bloated' according to another professional examiner[5]. His body also had a broken rib and bones, leg and head* severed from the body[9], and almost the whole front of his body missing; bits of pebble wrapped into his body by the embalmers, also bird legs, and a stray big toe from another human; he appears to have died at the age of around 40-50 with no clear cause of death. This damage is far in excess of what one would expect even as a result of grave robbery, and is far worse than other kings' mummies. See Chapter 4 for the detail.

■ AMENHOTEP III MUMMY CONTAINS PEBBLES

A detailed movement-by-movement of the unwrapping of the mummy is described by Grafton Smith on those pages[9], with relatively clear monochrome photographs also, and on this point it says,

> *"Then another bandage wound around the legs spirally down to the feet and then back again beyond the knees, there were pieces of pebble in this bandage."*

■ AMENHOTEP III MUMMY CONTAINS STRAY HUMAN BIG TOE

Smith[9] gives a further detailed movement-by-movement of the unwrapping of the mummy, with detailed photographs also, and on this point it says,

> *"The broken fragments of the body were held together by means of three bandages tied around them. Among the lumps of resin-impregnated linen inside the body cavity were found the leg bone of a fowl and another bird's limb bone, a human great toe, and a left ulnar and radius."*

■ AMENHOTEP III TOMB NOT RESPECTED, DECORATED, NOR FINISHED

Experts have been disappointed by the poverty and unimaginative character of his original tomb at WV22, while the carving out of the shafts and rooms is nonetheless well done and such decoration as there is, is of a very high quality, maybe being worked upon during his lifetime.

None of the painted scenes has been engraved, strangely. You get the impression that the work was done in haste and a limited time, with little incentive to give it the usual attention and respect, especially considering the magnificence of his reign. Chapter 4 has the detail.

■ CROWN PRINCE DJHUTMOSE (FIRSTBORN) DIED WHILE YOUNG

Amenhotep III's eldest son died before him (as a young firstborn); the same fact as is explained fully in the Hebrew *Bible* at Exodus 12:29. He was only aged about 10 or 11 years.

> *"In the middle of the night, Jehovah struck down all the firstborn in the land of Egypt, from the firstborn of Pharoah who sat on the throne to the firstborn of ..."*

Crown Prince Djhutmose, the firstborn son of Amenhotep III, and who died mysteriously in young teen years.

'Crown Prince Djhutmose' mummy is thought[10] to be the boy in tomb KV35 alongside the mummy of his mother, Queen Tiye (whose identity has been proven by DNA tests), and in close proximity to his father Amenhotep III. His relationship to Amenhotep III is proven by the sarcophagus of his cat (aptly named *Ta-miu*, 'the cat'), and seven jar lid inscriptions, in the Louvre.

He would have been the next Pharoah instead of Akhenaten.

The limestone sarcophagus of his she-cat Ta-miu gives his royal titles thus: *"Crown Prince, Overseer of the Priests of Upper & Lower Egypt, High Priest of Ptah in Memphis and Sem-priest (of Ptah)."* A small statuette of the Prince is in the *Louvre* and a mummiform figure of him is in Berlin.

The cat sarcophagus proves beyond reasonable doubt that he was the eldest son of Amenhotep III, since it displays his current title 'Crown Prince.'

Akhenaten then succeeded him to the throne, as the second-born son!

■ BURIAL OF 'CROWN PRINCE DJHUTMOSE' WITH PARENTS

The close proximity of the mummies of firstborn Crown Prince DJhutmose with his mother and father in KV35, and his mysterious death at such a young age could hardly be closer to our Hebrew Exodus expectations, of the burial of a young boy so dramatically killed. Each detail of this fits amazingly well with the expectations of the Exodus account.

The sarcophagus of the pet cat belonging to young Crown Prince Djhutmose who was the firstborn son of Amenhotep III but who died mysteriously at around age 11 - 15.

The Crown Prince's mummy is buried alongside his mother.

■ SUDDEN EMPHASIS ON 'TRUTH'

How appropriate it was that the slogan for the new Aten religion was "Living in Truth", and the new capital called " 'the Aten' Is Found", especially in view of the likely disorientation of the people's faith after the Exodus and Plagues. Akhenaten himself seems initially to purposely blend the status and identity of the *'Maat'* ('the truth', 'straight', 'righteous') into the single now more emphatic *'The* Aten' deity, whilst banning virtually all other deities. In the contemporary tomb of Ramose, Akhenaten is shown side by side with the goddess Maat.

■ UNCHALLENGED DESTRUCTION OF FALSE RELIGIONS

It is well known and demonstrated that Akhenaten later sent his hit-men out throughout the land, scrubbing out the references to plural 'gods', and any god name other than 'the Aten', closing their temples and re-directing their income directly to his own coffers too. These gods deserved to be in ruins!

The Hebrew *Bible* makes quite a prominent feature of the fact that the people of Egypt, and especially the royals, were to 'know' that their gods are useless. (Exodus 12:12 also 11:6, 10:16, 10:2 paraphrases)

> *"I will go through the land of Egypt and strike down every first-born ... and I will mete out punishments to all the gods of Egypt"*

> *"there shall be a loud cry in all of Egypt, such as has never been nor will ever be again."*

> *"Pharoah said... 'I have sinned against Yahweh your God and against you.'*

> *"that you may recount in the hearing of your sons and of your sons' sons how I made a mockery of the Egyptians and how I displayed my signs to them.'*

Yet this monumental decree met with no recorded rebellion; it seems that at the time it was obvious why such a massive change was justified... even Akhenaten's own personal name needed to be changed, as he had been born as Amen-Hotep.

■ AKHENATEN WAS THE SECOND-BORN

Akhenaten succeeded his father Amenhotep III as king, (this fact now also supported by recent DNA tests, published in the *American Journal of Medicine* in 2010) yet he was not the firstborn son. His elder brother, the 'Crown Prince Djhutmose [Thutmose]' evidently died young, probably aged 11, without becoming a ruler.

The Crown Prince then totally disappears from public records and appears to have died very late in Amenhotep III's reign. Akhenaten then succeeded him to the throne, evidently quite unprepared for this role.

In his work, *Amenhotep III: Uncles, Brothers, Sons and the Serapeum*, Aidan Dodson suggests that "*the interval between Prince Djhutmose' death and Amenophis IV's (Akhenaten's) accession was short.*"

■ AMENHOTEP III WAS A GREAT BUILDER

Amenhotep III was a great builder, lived a relatively long time (38 yr reign); so this fits the Exodus account of a highly successful, proud Pharoah, who needed a lot of bricks (made with straw!)... some of these bricks have been found, and are on display in the *British Museum,* also in *New York's Met Art Museum,* and in the *Cairo Museum.* Also, there are reliefs from that time which display huge amounts of building and brick-making being done, with slave labour.

■ EGYPT'S MISSING GOLD

Several Amarna letters say "*as gold is as dust in the land of my brother (Egypt)...*" yet it seems that Akhenaten was trying to preserve whatever gold remained in Egypt by greatly reducing the amount of gold in traditional gifts, for example the two gold statues sent to a king in Canaan, which statues apparently were expected to be solid gold, instead of thinly gold-plated wood! This reminds us of the references that tell of the Hebrews being given vast amounts of gold when they left Egypt. (Exodus 11:2,3 also 12:35,36)

"*all the men and women should ask their neighbour for objects of silver and gold... Moses was greatly esteemed in the land of Egypt among Pharoah's courtiers and the people.*"

"*the Israelites.. asked the Egyptians for silver and gold as well as clothing. .. they let them have their request, thus they stripped the Egyptians*"

Royal collar from the Amarna period, with notable lack of gold.

There is ample evidence that the Hebrews had huge amounts of gold after this time; the 'golden calf', the tabernacle and later temple(s) were lavishly furnished with gold, also the ark of the Covenant and many other utensils, yet they were previously only unpaid slaves in Egypt, living far from the source of gold production in Nubia, which was at the other (south) end of Egypt.

Gradually the new Amarna-based government would probably have been able to rebuild stocks of gold adequate for domestic consumption, and this is evidenced by the euergetistic golden gifts, necklaces and jewellery at royal Amarna events. This would serve to placate the populace, and maybe disguise the huge loss of gold already suffered. The actual quantity may not have been huge. Some scrap gold pieces have been found in the ruins of Akhet-Aten, in fact; either they were the loot of a thief or the raw materials of a jeweller or goldsmith. This has been an isolated find, however.

■ POWER OF 'ATEN' SUN FEATURED, RATHER THAN THE DISK ITSELF

Akhenaten featured not the actual physical Sun disk in his new monotheistic worship, but the light emanating from the circular sun... the rays shown with human-like hands on the end of each, as if recognising a god who could actually make things happen powerfully, even save or take away life, and should be the One now recognisable as superior to all their gods now discredited specifically in plagues that intentionally matched each individual quality of their major gods, showing them as artificial and useless, their status ruined.

Superimposed on 'the Aten' is the uraeus (rampant snake), a symbol of sovereignty.

■ THE TIMING OF THE NEW GRAPHIC PORTRAYAL OF 'THE ATEN'

Most significantly, this portrayal of 'power rays' with hands and *ankhs* starts specifically immediately after the Exodus and Akhenaten's taking up the kingship; although 'the Aten' had been a god since early times, he had until this moment been portrayed as a falcon-headed man. Some of the new Aten's rays displayed hands holding out *ankhs* (life) to the royals, but most rays seem to be indicating this god's wide-ranging ability to take real action, affecting human lives. It could be that the beliefs of the royal-household-educated Moses and the *"highly esteemed"* predecessor (a royal favourite) Joseph (who some think was possibly 'Yuya'; see discussion later) were the main influencers for this belief, in addition to the astounding effect of the plagues and the Exodus. More on this in Chapters 5 and 6.

A small stela found at Thebes, displaying an early Aten image in the form of the sun's rays.

This style of representation of the Aten was a major change from the falcon-headed human previously used in most reliefs.

■ AKHENATEN STRUGGLED TO KEEP PEOPLE HAPPY AFTER HIS FATHER'S DEATH

In only Year 3 of his reign Akhenaten hosted a 'sed' (*ḥb-sd*) feast, at Luxor, featuring the 'sun disc is found' (at his new Gem-pa-Aten temple) in an attempt to raise the spirit of the people ('seds' were usually in the king's 30th year). *"The Sun disc is found"* was the title of his new temple at Gem-pa-Aten. He quickly built four huge new palaces in that area, all featuring 'the Aten' as the god, whilst initially allowing a few other gods to continue in favour, as a side show. It seems there was a need for him to make a massive gesture to restore hope, or to provide a major new focus for a seemingly sad population.

■ ANCIENT HISTORIANS MATCH AKHENATEN WITH THE EXODUS

(See Chapter 7) The Jewish/Roman historian Josephus quotes Manetho with regard to early Egyptian events. Manetho was a third-century BCE historian and priest of Egypt, who wrote his *'History of Egypt' ['Aegyptiaca']*. Unfortunately, Manetho is viewed as particularly unreliable and inaccurate, but he did make one of the most complete attempts at listing the full history of early Egypt, from whatever temple scrolls he had access to.

Manetho says that the Exodus Pharoah was 'Amenophis' (the Greek equivalent of Amenhotep) and that Moses lived at the same time. This Pharoah is thought to be Amenhotep III[11]. Although there can be doubt about the names used by Manetho, he cannot have made up the account of religious rebellion and the link with Moses, who he says was Egyptian (as he nominally was, though not by birth); oral traditions will have persisted and no doubt formed the basis of his account. Other historians including Josephus, Africanus and the highly regarded Eusebius similarly believed that Moses and the Exodus belong in the pre-Amarna age.

Donald B Redford recognised Manetho's 'Osarseph' story as related to the Amarna religious revolution. He says:

> *"... a number of later independent historians, including Manetho, date Moses and the bondage to the Amarna period"*[12]

The obvious destruction of Egypt's international status and most of its infrastructure during the Amarna age, and just prior to it, is not easily explained in any other way than the monumental result of the ten plagues and the Exodus.

■ INFLUENCE OF MONOTHEISM BY MOSES

Akhenaten would very likely have been influenced by some notable monotheist characters that the Hebrew *Bible* reliably describes in great detail, and who were living at this time or in recent memory; firstly, Joseph who had much earlier infiltrated the Courts of Pharoah to the very top and was greatly respected... he worshipped the Hebrew God known in English as 'Jehovah' or sometimes 'Yahweh', from the ancient vowel-less Hebrew.

Also, Moses would have shown the greatly superior powers of YHWH in discrediting the gods of Egypt in the 10 plagues, including the miraculous killing of the male firstborn, and of course the Exodus itself with its evidently supernatural intervention in the parting of the Red Sea, the destruction of the Egyptian army and its Pharoah, and the consequent saving of the Hebrews.

Also Moses' mother was used by the Court of Pharoah to raise her own son Moses within Egyptian high society, and she can be assumed to have had some Hebrew influence on others in the household. The name "YHWH" is recorded as being actually spoken many times by both Pharoah and Moses in their negotiations; See Exodus 10:3, 7, 8, 10, 11, 16, 24, 25, 26 & 14:7, 25; also at Exodus 3:18, 19, 20, 21 and 4:22, 5:17

■ INFLUENCE OF MONOTHEISM BY JOSEPH

Joseph and Yuya look tantalisingly to be one and the same person, and (some think) may be Akhenaten's grandfather. His mummy is very well preserved and his Semitic nose seems quite distinctively Hebrew in character. Joseph's name (Yu-Seph) is comprised of Yu (from Yah or Jah, an abbreviation of Jehovah [YaHWeH]) and Seph (close to the Egyptian name given to Joseph by the Egyptians in Genesis 41:40-45, Zaph-e-nath-pa-neah which means 'Revealer of Hidden Things' referring to his prophetic dreams and astounding abilities.)

Josephus, the 1st-century Jewish-Roman historian, quotes from native Egyptian historian Manetho (3rd century BCE) and refers to Joseph as Osar-Seph ('Vizier Seph') who in the time of Amenhotep III *"prohibited the worship of the many Egyptian gods"*!

However, the burial procedures for Joseph do not match Yuya's, but it could be that Yuya was a very close relative of Joseph, possibly a son, with similar high office... this may better fit the generation differential also. The coffin of Yuya features several 'pagan' gods, which would have been anathema to Joseph.

Therefore although Yuya and Joseph cannot be the same person (more on this in Chapter 6), it is exceedingly likely that Joseph would have been an early influence on the royal family in their understanding of a religious alternative.

■ VIZIERS QUITE LIKELY TO BE MONOTHEISTIC SUPPORTERS

Prime ministers ('viziers', of which there were generally at least two at any time) include several characters who could quite likely have been Semitic, and already at least sympathetic to the Israelite belief in one god, through state contact with the Hebrews Moses, Aaron and even Joseph, or Queen Tiye who is also thought to have been very positive about monotheism.

Viziers like Aper-el (his Semitic name literally means 'servant of El') were advising Akhenaten at a very early time in his reign, and effectively gave for-eign support to the monotheistic ideology of 'the Aten'. See the many writings of Zivie and Gessler-Lohr on excavations at the Saqqara tombs, including the undisturbed tomb of vizier Aper-el from the Amarna period.

It must also be remembered that the population of Egypt around this time included a very high percentage of Hebrews; some say 33%, others 50%.

■ UNFAIR TAGS: 'HERETIC', 'ATHEIST', 'PACIFIST'

Archaeologists and historians are not necessarily best equipped to decide on terms like 'heretic', 'atheist' or even 'pacifist'... a deeper insight into religious perspectives is needed.

Without the Hebrew *Bible*, it would be difficult to understand the motivation(s) of Akhenaten, and this is an obvious gap in current traditional archaeological theories.

It is easy to see the surface of the matter, that Akhenaten did not send an army into Canaan (rather like a pacifist may behave, except that a pacifist would make more of an effort at negotiation with an enemy, or with his allies for that matter); that he did not really send any significant gold in that period (what a scoundrel! ... was he callous, or supremely un-caring, or distracted?); that he inexplicably and quite suddenly dismantled the entire framework of organized religion in the empire and focused on just one very different god; that a major Pharoah suddenly died tragically, his body being ripped open and mixed with pebbles and crud; and that his firstborn son died very young, without any visible cause; that there was a sudden governmental emphasis on 'truth', in all matters... yes, the surface of the matter is almost unanimous-ly agreed, but the reasons can only be discerned by linking all these facts, and many more details, with the reliable but astonishing accounts related in Scripture. Truth is stranger than fiction, after all!

The Hebrew *Bible* can be shown to be the only fitting explanation for the radi-cal actions of Akhenaten and his advisers.

■ THE PASSOVER HAS BEEN CELEBRATED BY THE JEWS EVER SINCE THE EXODUS

The fact that the 'Jews' (Hebrews) have celebrated the Passover, with all its deep symbolisms generated by the Exodus, ever since their escape into the Sinai wilderness around 1500 BCE (we are not debating the chronology here), surely proves that this was a *real* event and that the significant features of their annual celebration are based on solid collective experience handed down through the centuries; the 'bread of distress', the 'blood on the door-posts', the Passover ('saving') Lamb, the precise timing, the re-enactment of what happened, the bitter greens, the promise to Abraham...

■ CHRISTIAN ADOPTION

This same celebration was carried forward into Christianity when the Christ himself used it as the basis of the Lord's Evening Meal (wrongly re-named 'Easter' with a massive and inappropriate pagan overlay of eggs, rabbits, and buns in many churches), to be held at exactly the same annual time, with some similar symbolisms and references, especially of unleavened bread. Christ thus viewed the Passover and the Exodus as quite definitely historical.

One of many bricks that have been found, bearing the cartouches of Amenhotep III and clearly comprised of straw as well as mud.

■ EGYPTOLOGY CHRONOLOGY IS NOTORIOUSLY UNRELIABLE & DEBATED

(See Chapter 7 of this book). This leaves adequate room for the above proposal; the so-called *'New Chronology'*[13] and especially Tim Mahoney's film *Patterns of Evidence: The Exodus*[14] gives a much better fit to the other evidence here presented, but I am not hung up on any particular dates; merely the circumstantial evidence.

Map of
the area relevant
to the Amarna Letters
showing some of the
place names
mentioned

HITTITE EMPIRE

MEDITERRANEAN SEA

Ugarit

MITANNI

Ashur

Kadesh

Cyprus
Alashiya

Byblos

AMURRU

Sidon

Tyre

Hazor

Jericho

Jerusalem

DEAD SEA

Babylon

Gaza

Lachish

El-Arish

CANAAN

MOAB

GOSHEN

Giza

Heliopolis

AMORITES

Sakkara

Memphis (Cairo)

LOWER EGYPT

Sinai

Akhet-Aten (Amarna)

RED SEA

NILE

Abydos

Karnak

(Waset)Thebes

Luxor

Valley of Kings

Edfu

Elephantine

Gebel Silsila

UPPER EGYPT

Soleb (south from here)

KUSH

NUBIA

Chapter 2

THE AMARNA LETTERS

Egypt's missing army

Egypt's missing gold

The tragic death of the previous Pharoah

Preview

The 'Amarna Letters', or Tablets, feature extremely prominently the total *lack of an Egyptian army* specifically at the time of the start of Akhenaten's reign, and evidently for some years after that.

Also prominent on a huge number of the pleading letters is the almost *total lack of gold gifts* which had previously been abundant during the reign of Amenhotep III.

Mention is also made of the *"tragic loss" of the previous Pharoah* (Amenhotep III), accompanied by great grief.

Letters written to the mother of an evidently too-young new Pharoah indicate a sudden and unexpected death of the previous Pharoah, and an unprepared successor. This fits too with the situation where the intended successor, *the firstborn son, was not in a position* to take up rulership.

When added to the separate evidence that Akhenaten was in fact the *second-born son and secondary heir,* and that he famously viewed the *gods as useless,* actually taking the unprecedented political step of *dismantling virtually the entire discredited god network,* as well as evidence that *his father's death seems extremely violent* and also possibly water-related, the conclusion powerfully supports the Exodus account.

The startling facts, context and subjective perspectives revealed in the Amarna Letters can surely be explained by the sequence of events outlined in considerable detail in the book of 'Exodus' in Hebrew Scripture.

THE AMARNA LETTERS, or Tablets, are cuneiform clay tablets all found in, surprisingly enough, a room called 'The Room of the Records of the Palace of the Pharoah' (a plaque reading this way is in the *Museum of Fine Arts, Boston*) amid the ruins of an ancient desert city in remote middle Egypt. That city was never actually called Amarna; that title dates back only to the 18th century when an explorer coined the site name based on a local tribal name, Beni-Amran and a nearby village known as Et Til el Amarna. The original city name, from the second millennium BCE, was Akhet-Aten; we shall refer to it as Akhet or Amarna to avoid confusion with the similar word Akhenaten, the personal name of its king and builder.

There are 382 tablets in various collections, primarily in the *British Museum* (95), Berlin (203), Cairo (50), Paris *Louvre* (7), and others held privately.

The letters were almost all written by relatively minor subordinate kings or vassals of the Levant (Mitanni, Hatti, Jerusalem, Beirut, Byblos, Syria (*Assyria*), Phoenicia, Palestine and Babylon) to Akhenaten; a few were written to his father Amenhotep III, and one or two to Queen Tiye, the mother of Akhenaten and wife of Amenhotep III. Some were written by Akhenaten, but most of these were never sent. The tablets would have been delivered to or from Egypt mostly by human messenger, the original 'E' mail!

A typical Amarna Letter of which 382 have been found, to date.

Most of them refer to the total lack of Egyptian army, as well as the lack of gold which had previously been shared profusely.

The language is mostly a 'quaint and archaic'[1] Akkadian cuneiform, using many words and expressions which were not in common usage at the time, but reflected an older manner, with some East Semitic endings and in-fixes.

They have been numbered, originally around the year 1915 by *Knudtzon*, a Norwegian Assyrian scholar. The numbering generally features two sections; the 'foreign powers' in order of geographical origin, counter-clockwise from Babylon [1-14 is Babylonia; 15-16 Assyria; 17,19-30 Mitanni (Syria); 31-32 Arzawa (Turkey); 33-40 Alasia (Cyprus); 41-44 Hatti (Turkey)] followed by the Syrian and Palestine vassal state letters and inventories numbered from North to South, with some recognition of chronological order where this can be determined. The prefix 'EA' represents 'El Amarna', strangely enough!

Amazingly, the letters were almost all found in 1887 by a peasant woman scratching in the ancient Amarna earth for some '*sebakh*' to fertilise her garden. At the time, no-one thought they had any worth; some thought they were forgeries, and she parted with them readily for the equivalent of ten pence.

The importance of the letters has increased with the years and new discoveries; they can now be viewed as "one of most valuable collections in world."

Translating the letters began with *Percy Handcock* 1920 (out of copyright), and *Mercer's* English in 1939, including 12 additional letters; then *Moran & Albright* when in 1948 they originally produced a part work; then *Moran* in French in 1987; also *Rainey and Zipora Cochavi* (1989 & 1996) in Hebrew, French and English, and *Moran* in English 1992.

For a comprehensive translation of the letters, and scholarly background and detail, see *William Moran, 'The Amarna Letters'* (in English, 1992) published by *The Johns Hopkins University Pre*ss.

Matching verses from the Hebrew *Bible:*

EGYPT'S MISSING ARMY:

The Scriptures state that the entire military brigade that chased the Hebrews across the Red Sea perished in their entirety, even the Pharoah himself:

Exodus 14:4, 7, 9, 17, 18, 23, 25, (and especially verse 28) & 15:4

> *"Pharoah... will chase after them... all his army..."*

> *"He took 600 chosen chariots and all the other chariots of Egypt..."*

> *"all the chariot horses of Pharoah and his horsemen and his army..."*

> *"Pharoah and all his army, his war chariots, and his horsemen."*

> *"all Pharoah's army, his war chariots, and his horsemen... into the sea."*

> *"wheels off their chariots so they were driving them with difficulty..."*

> *"The returning waters covered the war chariots and the horsemen and all of Pharoah's army who had gone into the sea after them. Not so much as one among them was allowed to survive."*

> *"Pharoah's chariots and his army He has cast into the sea, his finest warriors have sunk into the Red Sea."*

Also **Psalm 136:15** states that this included the Pharoah:

> *"He shook off Pharoah and his army into the Red Sea... He struck down great kings... He killed mighty kings..."*

... thus there was not an army remaining in Egypt, and Amenhotep III died tragically, his body mutilated by his mode of death in the sea.

EGYPT'S MISSING GOLD:

The Scriptures state that the Egyptian people voluntarily gave their gold and silver to the departing Hebrews; **(Exodus 11:2,3 also 12:35,36)**

> *"all the men and women should ask their neighbor for articles of silver and gold... Moses had become highly esteemed in the land of Egypt among Pharoah's servants and the people."*

> *"the Israelites.. asked the Egyptians for articles of silver and gold as well as clothing. .. they gave them what they asked for, and they stripped the Egyptians"*

EGYPT'S MISSING FIRSTBORN SUCCESSOR PHAROAH:

The Scriptures state specifically that the Egyptian successor prince, being the firstborn son, was killed in the tenth plague; **(Exodus 12:29)**

> *"Then at midnight, Jehovah smote all the firstborn in Egypt, from the firstborn of Pharoah that sat on his throne to the captive..."*

A small selection, showing the fit with Exodus

See especially **Letter EA29** by Tushratta the king of Mitanni; the condolences for the sudden death of the previous Pharoah, who is said to have "gone to his fate". It reads: *"When my brother went to his fate it was reported. When I heard what was reported... I grieved, saying, "Let even me be dead, or let 10,000 be dead in my country, and in my brother's country 10,000 as well, but let my brother, whom I love and who loves me, be alive as long as heaven and earth. I didn't sleep, I didn't eat any food, I didn't drink any drink."*

Letter EA26 is a letter written to the widow of the dead Pharoah, Queen Tiye, as though she were in charge while a new young son is not yet fully effective as the next Pharoah.

Letters EA29 and many others refer to the highly remarkable and relevant lack of gold in that period; whereas the gold gifts had previously been profuse under the leadership of Amenhotep III, there is at best a minimal presence of gold in the supplies sent to the claimants.

Letters EA114, 251 and many others accuse Akhenaten of 'negligence', many of them speaking of false promises or total military or political inaction on his part.

Letters EA 125, 206 and many others speak of archers, garrisons, soldiers or commissioners being promised, but that the supplicants must 'guard themselves' in the meantime.

Letter EA 126 and others refer to earlier times of plenty with Amenhotep III.

Letter EA 272 and many others describe the war developments with the Apiru (Hapiru/ Habiru).

Letter EA 318 and others talk of a coalition with the Apiru; the 'Suteans and robbers' as well as whole communities who voluntarily joined them, or surrended at their threat.

Letter EA 254 hints at a certain cynicism on the writer's part, with gushing, quite evidently false, humility and subservience to the Pharoah. EA16 also, from Assur-Uballit, is quite cheeky, even scandalous, in demanding more gold as a gift.

Some letters relate to the reign of Amenhotep III, specifically around the start of his 30th yr [EA17, 19, 20, 21, 24, 25, 23]: others relate to the first year of King 'Tut', after Akhenaten's reign of over 16 years.

Previous Egyptology authors of the last 150 years, both scholarly and otherwise, have either delved deep into the Akkadian grammar and technical aspects of the Letters or proposed quite loose fitting hypotheses regarding Joseph, Moses and other characters. There is now a need to step back and review the whole corpus of evidence, increased wonderfully as it has been in recent years with new finds, DNA analysis and tomb exploration... especially to compare the letters with the original account of the Exodus in the book of that same name. The fit is amazing.

Who is Who?

Abdi-Asirta; leader of Amurru, a new state in Canaan/Syria

Abdi-Heba; soldier-leader in Jerusalem

Abdi-Milki; ruler-mayor of Sashimi, near Damascus

Abdi-Risa; ruler of Enisasi, in Lebanon

AbiMilki (Abi-Milku); Tyre king

Akhenaten; son of Amenhotep III. Known (earlier) as Amenhotep IV.

Akizzi; king of Qatna (Homs, Syria)

Amanappa; an Egyptian official

Amenhotep III; father of Akhenaten. One of the greatest Pharoahs

Amenophis 4; Greek name for Amenhotep IV, Akhenaten

Aperel; vizier early in reign of Amenhotep III also early in Akhenaten

Apiru; a marauding tribe. Some think these were the 'Hebrews'

Artamanya; a Mitanni senior

Arzawaija of Ruhiza

Ashur-Uballit; an Assyria king

Ay; later rebel & king

Aziru; leader of Amurru, son of Abdi-Asirta

Baalat; a mythological goddess, the "Lady of Byblos"

Baiawa; leader in Gaza

Bajadi; a minor leader

Biridija; Megiddo king

Biryawaza; mayor of Damascus

Burna-Buriash; Babylon king

'Chamberlain' Tutu; probably in charge of Records at Amarna

Dagantakala; an early Philistine

Dijate; a minor leader in Canaan

Etakkama; mayor of Qadesh (Kadesh)

Gilukhepa; secondary queen of Amenhotep III, daughter of Shuttarna and sister of Tushratta

Henattaneb; daughter of Amenhotep III

Iapahi; Gezer mayor

Isis; daughter of Amenhotep III

Labaya; leader of Shechem

"Lady of Byblos"; Baalat, a mythological goddess; like Hathor-Isis

Milkili; Gezer mayor (Carmel area)

'Mimmureya'; see Amenhotep III

Nimmureya; Nibmuareya'; see Amenhotep III

Naphurure-ya; Amenhotep IV.

Rib-Hadda; leader in Gubla (probably Byblos, Jebal)

Satatna; king of Acco (Akka) (Acre)

Sitamen; wife & daughter of Amenhotep III

Suppiluliuma; Hittite king

Suwardata; king of Qiltu (northeast Canaan).

Tadu-Heba (Tadukhipa); daughter of Tushratta; minor wife of Amenhotep III; also wife to Akhenaten

Tiye; wife of Amenhotep III. Mother of Akhenaten. From Mitanni. Daughter of Yuya (chariot boss)

Tushratta; Leader of Mitanni

Yapah-Hadda; mayor of Baruta (Beirut)

Yuya; served both Pharoahs

Zimredda; mayor of Lachish (Lakish)

Zitrijara; a minor Hittite leader

Here is a part paraphrase in English of those Amarna Letters that have more relevance and context to Akhenaten's handling of international affairs:

I have generally used William Moran's[1] first two lines of heading, to assist in further reading from his translations and extensive notes.

EA 7

Babylon king Burna-Buriash to Amenhotep IV ('Naphurure-ya');
Most of the gold is missing

"My brother should make a personal check, then he should seal and send it to me; certainly my brother did not check the earlier shipment of gold; when I put the 40 minas of gold into the kiln **not even [10?] I swear appeared.**"

EA 8

Babylon king Burna-Buriash to Amenhotep IV
Merchants murdered!

"Canaan is your country...in your country **I have been despoiled... bring them to account** and make compensation... put to death the men who put my servants to death."

EA 9

Babylon king Burna-Buriash to Amenhotep IV
Lack of gold!

"From the time my ancestors made a mutual friendship they sent beautiful gifts and refused no request; my brother now sent me 2 minas of gold as my gift.. now if gold is plentiful send me as much as your ancestors sent, but if it is scarce, send me half. **Why have you sent me just two minas of gold?** At the moment my work on a temple is extensive."

It is essential to read at least these abbreviated Letters to appreciate the loss of the Egyptian army and gold.

EA 10

Babylon king Burna-Buriash to Amenhotep IV
Is this really gold?

"I am one for whom nothing is scarce, and you are one for whom nothing is scarce. As for the 20 minas of gold sent here, it was not all there; when they put it in the kiln **not 5 minas of gold appeared, and when it cooled it looked like ashes**... was it identified as gold? ... friends with each other...

EA 11

Babylon king Burna-Buriash to Amenhotep IV ('Naphurure-ya')
Egyptian royal parent mourned, and we need more gold please!

"... of your **father had been mourned**, I sent Hua my messenger and an interpreter to you. I wrote saying 'a daughter of the king who was once taken to your father; let them take another to you. And **you replied saying "... my father was mourned** ... that woman ... she died in a plague ... wrote saying 'that woman may be taken.'" ' "

"After **your father sent here much gold, what was more lavish than this**, so in the palace of my ancestor what was missing? That neighbouring kings may hear it said 'the gold is much; among the kings there is brotherhood, amity, peace and friendship'. ... As soon as possible let them take to me much gold that is yours alone; let them take to me much gold! By the end of this year I wish to bring the work to completion."

EA 16

Assyria king Ashur-Uballit to Amenhotep IV
"Gold is as dust.. but where is it?"

"I send as your gift a beautiful royal chariot and 2 white horses, and a seal of lapis lazuli."

"Is such a present that of a Great king? Gold in your country is dirt; one simply gathers it up. **Why are you so sparing of it?** I am engaged in building a new palace; send me as much gold as needed for its adornment. ... When my ancestor Assurnadinahhe wrote to Egypt 20 talents of gold were sent to him... and when the king of Hanigalbat wrote to your father in Egypt he sent 20 talents of gold to him. I am the equal of Hanigalbat but you sent me [...] of gold and it is not enough... If your purpose is graciously one of friendship then send me much gold, and this is your house.

The following two letters are strange, in apparently complaining to Amenhotep III about his gold; it could be that by the time the gold arrived in Canaan, Akhenaten was actually the king, or that the comprehensive giving of gold to the Hebrews had already happened.

EA 20

Mitanni king Tushratta (Queen Tiye's father) to Amenhotep III ('Mimmureya');
It doesn't look like gold

"My messengers will bring [his] wife to my brother and when they show her to my brother he will note this; she has become very mature, and she has been fashioned according to my brothers desire."

"With regard to the gold that my brother sent, I gathered all my foreign guests … they wept very much, and said 'are all these gold'? They do not look like gold. In Egypt, gold is more plentiful than dust; besides, my brother loves you very much; but if there be someone whom he loves then he would not give such things to him."

"My brother will consider whether I was somewhat distressed or not. "

EA 24

Mitanni king Tushratta to Amenhotep III; written in Hurrian language
Some gold & ivory statues please

"One more thing I wish to say; and may my brother heed it. The things that Artatama my grandfather did for your father are […] and with just a single dispatch of mine I have done 10 times as much; … thus shall I deal loyally with my brother, thus I shall be most loving."

"And for the horses (that I sent) **my brother did not reward me with gold the way my forefathers were rewarded**; my brother has not given me the equivalent of what he gave my father. May my brother make me rich in respect to the kings, my vassals, and other lands, with much gold. … May my brother make a solid gold image of his wife, my sister. Also I have asked for a solid gold image of my daughter; I know my brother loves me very much! – from his heart. But I know that gold is very plentiful in his land. May he not distress my heart. Maybe he could also make an ivory image, as I shall speak to my goddess Sauska of Nineveh."

"So it should be; 'This molten gold image is Tadu-Heba daughter of Tushratta the Lord of Mittani whom he gave as wife of Mimmureya the Lord of Egypt. Mimmureya commissioned this molten gold image and full of love sent it to Tushratta."

EA 26

Mitanni king Tushratta to Tiye, widow of Amenhotep III ('Mimmureya')

Missing gold statues

This important letter hints strongly that Amenhotep III has died, hence the letter is written to his widow Tiye, and shows strong disappointment that the young new king Naphurureya (Akhenaten/Akhenamun/Amenophis IV), the second-born son of Tiye, has **sent statues of wood instead of solid gold**.

This letter has a side note that it arrived at Waset (Thebes), in "Year 2" (unclear, but generally accepted), and uses the throne name of Akhenaten (Neferkheperu-re). See page 108 of this book for more detail and an illustration.

"**To Tiye, the mistress of Egypt**: from Tushratta the king of Mittani... **For your household, for your son**, may all go well. For Tadu-Heba my daughter, your daughter-in-law, may all go well."

"You are the one that knows that I myself always **showed love to Mimmureya your (late) husband** and Mimmureya on the other hand always showed love to me. And the things that I would write and say to Mimmureya your husband and the things that Mimmureya on the other hand would always write to me and say, you are the one who knows much better than all the others the things that we said to one another. No one else knows them as well."

"And now are you yourself said to Keliya, 'say to your Lord, "Mimmureya my husband always showed love to your father, and maintained it for you. He did not forget his love for your father and he did not cut off the embassies that he had been accustomed to sending one after the other. And now you are the one that must not forget your love for Mimmureya. **Increase it for Naphurureya (Akhenaten)** and maintain it for him. **You must keep on sending 'embassies of joy' one after the other; do not cut them off** ."

"I will not forget the love for Mimmureya your husband. More than ever before, at this very moment, I show 10 times - more love to Naphurureya, your son. You know the words of Mimmureya your husband, **yet you did not send all my greeting gift that your husband ordered to be sent to me. I had asked your husband for statues of solid gold**, saying, 'May my brother send me as my gift, statues of solid cast gold and genuine lapis lazuli'. But Naphurureya **your son has sent plated statues of wood. With gold being as dust in your son's country, why have they been such a source of distress** that he has not given them to me? Is this love? I had said, Naphurureya my brother is going to treat me 10 times better than his father did". But now he has not given me even what his father was accustomed to give."

"Why have you not exposed before Naphurureya the words that you yourself, with your own mouth, said to me? If you do not expose them before him, and you keep silent, can anyone else know? Let Naphurureya give me statues of solid gold! He must cause me no distress whatsoever; let him treat me 10 times better than his father did, with love and evidence of esteem."

EA 27

Mitanni king Tushratta to Amenhotep IV
More missing gold statues & gold supplies

"Say to Naphurureya the king of Egypt, my brother, my son-in-law, whom I love and who loves me; thus Tushratta, great king, the king of Mitanni, your father-in-law, who loves you, your brother. For me all goes well. For you may all go well. For Tiye your mother, for your household, may all go well."

... "My brother said this, "Just as you always showed love to my father Mimmureya so now show love to me. After my brother is desirous of my love, shall I not be desirous of my brother's love? At this very moment I show you 10 times more love than I did to your father!"

"And your father Mimmureya, said this on his tablet; (when Mane brought the bride price, thus spoke my brother) "These goods that I have now sent are nothing, and my brother is not to complain. I have sent nothing. These goods that I have now sent you, I have sent to you with this understanding that, when my brother hands over my wife whom I have asked for, and they bring her here and I see her, then I will send you 10 times more than this."

"I also asked your father Mimmureya for statues of solid cast gold, one of myself and the second statue, a statue of Tadu-Heba, my daughter, and your father said, "Don't talk of giving statues just of solid cast gold; I will also give you ones made of lapis lazuli. I will give you along with the statues much additional gold and other goods beyond measure.

Every one of my messengers that were staying in Egypt saw all the gold for the statues with their own eyes. Your father himself recast the statues in the presence of my messengers, and he made them entirely of pure gold. My messengers saw with their own eyes that they were recast, and they saw with their own eyes that they were entirely of pure gold."

"He showed much additional gold, which was beyond measure and which he was sending to me. He said to my messengers, "See with your own eyes, here the statues, there much gold and goods beyond measure which I'm sending to my brother", and my messengers did see with their own eyes!"

"But **my brother has not sent the solid gold statues that your father was going to send**. You have sent plated ones of wood. "

"Yet there is nothing I know of in which I have failed my brother. Any day that I hear the greetings of my brother, that day I make a festive occasion."

"May my brother send me much gold. And with many goods may my brother honour me. In my brother's country gold is as plentiful as dust; may my brother cause me no distress."

EA 29

Mitanni king Tushratta to the son of Amenhotep III
Mourning for tragic death of Amenhotep III (Mimmureya)

"Mimmureya sent his messenger and put before me 7 sacks full of gold, and 1 ingot of gold weighing 1000 shekels. Plus Mimmureya your father made ... exceed, out of love.

Because he sent him promptly, he did not have the statues brought to me, but everything else was limitless. Thus Mimmureya, your father, did not permit that in any matter, even one, distress be caused to me."

"When **my brother Mimmureya went to his fate it was reported**. When I heard what was reported, nothing was allowed to be cooked in a pot. On that day I myself wept, and I sat on that day I took neither food nor water; **I grieved, saying, "Let even me be dead**, or let 10,000 be dead in my country and in my brothers country 10,000 as well, but let my brother whom I love and who loves me be alive as long as heaven and earth."

"But when they said that the oldest son of Mimmureya and Tiye is exercising the kingship in his place, then I spoke; 'Mimmureya my brother is not dead! His son must be ruling in his place; nothing is going to change from the way it was before."

"But when my brother (Naphurure-ya) first wrote to me, **my brother sent me statues made of wood! When I saw the gold that Mimmureya himself had promised, that it was not gold and that it was not solid**, then I was in greater pain than ever. I became angry and very hostile."

"Please now enquire carefully of your mother about the words that your mother herself spoke. I asked for statues of solid chased gold, and the object of my desire you have not sent. Should I be confident in you?"

EA 33

Alashiya (Cyprus) king to Pharaoh (Amenhotep IV ?)
A new king in Egypt

"To the king of Egypt, my brother: message of the king of Alashiya, your brother; for me all goes well. ... **I have heard that you are seated on the throne of your father's house**. You said, "Let us have transported back and forth **gifts of peace**. I have heard the greeting of my brother and ... have transported to you 10 talents of fine copper."

> *"In my brother's country gold is as plentiful as dust; may my brother cause me no distress"*

EA 35

Alashiya (Cyprus) king to Pharaoh
The hand of Nergal, and please pay for the timber.

"Say to the king of Egypt, my brother: ... My brother, I herewith send my messenger with your messenger to Egypt. I herewith send you 500 talents of copper. ... My brother do not be concerned that the amount of copper is small; behold, the hand of Nergal (pestilence? in Cyprus) is now in my country; he has slain all the men of my country and there is not a single copper worker. So my brother, do not be concerned. Send your messenger with my messenger immediately, and I will send you whatever copper you request. You are my brother. May you send silver in very great quantities; my brother give me the very best silver and then I will send you, my brother, whatever you request."

"Men of my country keep speaking to me about my timber that the king of Egypt receives from me. My brother, **give me the payment due**."

EA 41

Hittite king Suppululiuma to Pharoah
Hittite diplomacy

"Thus the sun, Suppululiuma, Great King, King of Hatti. Say to Huri-ya, the king of Egypt, my brother: ...

Why my brother have **you held back the presents that your father made to me** when he was alive? Now my brother you have ascended the throne of your father, and just as your father and I were desirous of peace between us, so now to you and I should be friendly with one another. The request that I expressed to your father I shall express to my brother also; let us be helpful to each other."

"Do not hold back anything that I asked of your father; as to the two statues of gold, one should be standing, one should be seated. And my brother, send me the two silver statues of women and a large piece of lapis lazuli. ...

I herewith send you a silver stag, and silver ram, 2 silver disks, 2 large trees."

EA 42

Hittite king to Pharaoh
Honour and status

"And now, as to the tablet that you sent me, why did you put your name over my name? And who is the one who now upsets the good relations between us, and is such conduct the accepted practice? My brother, did you write to me with peace in mind? And if you are my brother, why have you exalted your name, while I, for my part am thought of as a corpse! I have written the names, but **your name I will blot out**."

> *"I have heard that you are seated on the throne of your father's house... my brother has not sent the solid gold..."*

EA55

Qatna king Akizzi to Amenhotep III
Please send troops and ransom money

"Say to Namhur-ya (Nibmuareya), the son of the Sun, my Lord: message of Akizzi, your servant. I fall at the feet of my lord seven times. ...

From the time my ancestors were your servants, this country has been your country, Qatna has been your city, and I belong to my lord.

My Lord, when the troops and chariots of my lord have come here, food, strong drink, oxen, sheep, goats, honey and oil were produced for the troops and chariots of my lord.

My Lord, the whole country is in fear of your troops and chariots. If my Lord would take this country for his own country, then let my lord send this year his troops and chariots so that they may come here and all of Nuhasse belong to my lord. They would certainly take Aziru. **If the troops and chariots of my lord do not come forth this year** and fight, the country will be in fear of Aziru.

The king of Hatti has taken the fighting men of Qatna now; he has led them away out of the country of my lord; they now dwell outside of the country of my lord. May my lord send some ransom money for these men, and may my lord ransom them; as much as it may be, so I can hand over the money."

EA64

Amurru king Abdi-Asirta to Pharaoh
Protect us please, and women for the king

"Message of Abdi-Asirta, servant of the king. ... May my lord be informed that the war against me is severe, and may it seem good to the king, my lord, to **send a magnate to protect me**. Moreover, the king, my lord, has sent orders to me and I am heeding them; I heed all the orders of the king, my lord. I herewith send 10 women to you."

EA68

Byblos (Gubal) king to Pharaoh
Byblos under attack by Apiru; please send troops.

"Rib-Hadda (Ribaddi) says to his lord, king of all countries, Great King:

The war, however, of the Apiru forces against me is extremely severe, and so may the king, my lord, not neglect Sumur lest everyone be joined to the Apiru forces. ... The war against us is extremely severe, and so **may the king not neglect his cities.**"

EA69

Gubal king Rib-Addi to Egypt official
Archers needed

"Message of Rib-Hadda. ... You yourself know that my towns are threatening me, and I have not been able to make peace with them. Moreover, Magdalu and the forces of Kuasbat are at war with me, and there is no one who can rescue me from them. Moreover, on Appiha's reaching me there was an outcry against me ... **I urge with a loud cries the king, ... if archers come out this year** I will be able to make peace."

EA70

Gubal king Rib-Addi to Pharaoh
Request for Nubian troops

"Send me [x] Egyptians and men from Meluhha (Nubia, part of Egypt) just as you did to the kings to whom you gave chariots, so they can guard until the coming of the archers. May the king, my lord, know that the land of Amurru longs day and night for the coming of the archers. **The day the archers arrive**, the land will certainly be joined ... to the king my lord."

EA71

Gubal king Rib-Addi to Haia(?)
Appeal to a wise man to ask for archers

"To Haya, the vizier; Message of Rib-Hadda. **Why have you been negligent, not speaking to the king** so he will send archers to take Sumur? What is Abdi-Asirta, servant and dog, that he takes the land of the king for himself? What is his auxiliary force that it is strong? Through the Apiru his auxiliary force is strong. So send me 50 pairs of horses and 200 infantry that I may resist him in Sigata until the coming forth of the archers. ... what shall I be able to do?"

"I urge with loud cries..."

EA73

Gubal king Rib-Addi to Amanappa
Another request for more archers

"To Amanappa, my father; Message of Rib-Hadda, your son. ... **Why have you been negligent**, not speaking to the king, your lord, so that you may come out together with archers? **If they hear of archers coming out, they will abandon their cities** and desert. They are longing day and night for the coming out of the archers and they say, 'Let us join them'. All the mayors long for this to be done to Abdi-Asirta, since he sent a message to the men of Ammiya, 'Kill your lord and join the Apiru' "

EA74

Gubal king Rib-Addi (Rib-Hadda)to Pharaoh
Like a bird in a trap

"Rib-Hadda says to his Lord, king of all countries, Great King, King of Battle; ...

Do not be negligent of your servant. Behold, the war of the Apiru even against me is severe and, as the gods of the land are alive, our sons and daughters have gone since they have been sold in the land of Yarimuta for provisions to keep us alive. "For lack of a cultivator my field is like a woman without a husband." All my villages that are in the mountains or along the sea have been joined to the Apiru. Left to me are Gubla (Byblos) and two towns. After taking Sigata for himself, Abdi-Asirta said to the men of Ammiya, "Kill your leader and then you will be like us and at peace." ...

Accordingly they have made an alliance among themselves and, accordingly I am very, very afraid, since in fact there is no one who will save me from them. Like a bird in a trap so am I in Gubla (Byblos). **Why have you neglected your country? I have written like this to the palace but you do not heed** my words. Look Amanappa is with you. Ask him. He is the one that knows and has experienced the straits I am in. May the king heed the words of his servant. May he grant provisions for his servant and keep his servant alive so I may guard his loyal city, along with our lady and our gods for you. May the king visit his land and his servant. May he give thought to his land. Pacify your land! What can I do by myself? This is what I long for the day and night."

Amun Ra, one of the foremost old gods, and one of the most alienated by Akhenaten

EA75

Gubal (Byblos) king Rib-Addi to Pharaoh
Desperate political chaos

"Rib-Hadda says to his Lord, king of all countries: ... the War of the Apiru against me is severe. Our sons and daughters and the furnishings of houses are gone, since they have been sold in the land of Yarimuta for our provisions to keep us alive. I have written repeatedly to the palace because of the [illness] affecting me but there is no one who has looked at the words that keep arriving. **May the king give heed** to the words of his servant. The Apiru killed Aduna, the king of Irqata, but there was no one who said anything to Abdi-Asirta, so they go on taking territory for themselves. I am afraid. May the king also be informed that the king of Hatti has seized all the countries that were vassals of the king of Mittani. ... **Send archers**. Severe is..."

EA76

Gubal (Byblos) king Rib-Addi to Pharaoh
Large force needed; please reply!

"Rib-Hadda says to his Lord, king of all countries:

May the king know that the war of Abdi-Asirta against me is severe. He wants to take the two cities that have remained to me. He has just gathered together all the Apiru against Sigata and Ampi and he himself has taken those two cities. I said, 'There is no place where men can enter against him. He has seized... so send me a garrison of 400 men and [x] pairs of horses with all speed. It is thus that I keep writing to the Palace, **but you do not reply to me**. For years archers would come out to inspect the country, and yet now that the land of the king and Sumur, your garrison city, have been joined to the Apiru, **you have done nothing. Send a large force of archers** that it may drive out of the king's enemies and all lands be joined to the king. Moreover, you are a great lord. You must not neglect this message."

EA77

Gubal king Rib-Addi to Amanappa
Peasantry rebelling & Apiru attacking

"To Amanappa, my father: Message of Rib-Hadda, your son...

Why **have you been negligent**? You do not speak to you lord and so he will send you at the head of the archers to drive of the Apiru from the mayors. If this year **no archers** come out then all lands will be joined to the Apiru. If the king, **my lord, is negligent and there are no archers**, then let a ship fetch the men of [Gubla], your men, and the gods to bring them all the way to you so I can abandon [Gubla]. Look, I am afraid the peasantry will strike me down."

"May a large force come"

EA78

Gubal king Rib-Addi to Pharaoh
Request for a garrison

"Rib-Hadda says to his Lord, king of all countries:

Now only two towns remain to me, and even these he strives to take. Like a bird in a trap, so am I in Gubla (Byblos). May my lord heed the words of his servant. **Send me immediately ... a garrison**, 30 pairs of horses in the charge of ..."

EA79

Gubal king Rib-Addi to Pharaoh
At the brink

"Rib-Hadda says to his Lord, king of all countries:

Be informed that since Amanappa reached me all the Apiru have at the urging of Abdi-Asirta turned against me. May my lord heed the words of his servant. **Send me a garrison** to guard the city of the king until the archers come out. If there are no archers, then all lands will be joined to the Apiru. Listen! Since Bitarha was seized at the urging of Abdi-Asirta they have as a result been striving to take over Gubla (Byblos) and Batruna, and thus all lands would be joined to the Apiru. There are two towns that remain to me and they want to take them from the king. May my lord send a garrison to his two towns **until the archers come out**, and may something be given to me for their food. I have nothing at all. Like a bird in the trap, so am I in Gubla. Moreover if the king is unable to save me from his enemies, then all lands will be joined to Abdi-Asirta. What is he, the dog, that he takes the lands of the king for himself?"

EA81

Gubal king Rib-Addi to Pharaoh
Attempted assassination

"Rib-Hadda says to his Lord, king of all countries:

Gubla and Batruna remain to me, and he strives to take the two towns. He said to the men of Gubla, 'Kill your lord and be joined to the Apiru like Ammiya.' So they became traitors to me. A man with a bronze dagger attacked me, but I killed him... I am unable to go out to the countryside, and I have written to the palace but you do not reply to me. I was struck 9 times. Accordingly I fear for my life. I have written repeatedly to the palace, '**Do not be negligent. Why are you negligent** of the distress afflicting me? If within these 2 months **there are no archers** then ... may he not fall upon my city and take me. I have written to the palace. What am I to say to my peasantry?"

EA82

Gubal king Rib-Addi to Amanappa
Threat to abandon Byblos

"To Amanappa, my father: Message of Rib-Hadda, your son...

Are you unable to rescue me from Abdi-Asirta? All the Apiru are on his side, and as soon as the mayors hear anything they write to him. Accordingly, he is strong. You ordered me, 'Send your man to the palace, ... and I shall send him along with an auxiliary force until the archers come out to protect your life.' But I told you, 'I am unable to send him. Let not Abdi-Asirta hear about it or who would rescue me from him? You said to me, 'Send a ship to the land of Yarimata so silver and clothing can get out to you from them.' **All the men you gave me have run off.**

Is it not a fact that I sent my man to the palace, and he gave orders to a man and he attacked me with a bronze dagger. I was stabbed 9 times! ... If within 2 months **there are no archers**, I shall abandon the city and go off. ... Come with all haste."

EA83

Gubal king Rib-Addi to Pharaoh
Pleas and threats

"Rib-Hadda says to his Lord, king of all countries:

Why do you not send back a word to me so that I may know what I should do? I sent a man of mine to my lord, and both his horses were taken. The second man—a man of his—was taken, and a tablet of the king was not put in my man's hand. Listen to me! **Why are you negligent so that your land is being taken**? Let it not be said in the days of the commissioners, 'The Apiru have taken the entire country!' —you will not be able to take it back. Moreover**, I have written for a garrison and horses, but they are not given.** Send back words to me, or like Yapah-Hadda and Zimredda I will make an alliance with Abdi-Asirta and stay alive."

"I keep writing to the palace"

EA84

Gubal king Rib-Addi to Pharaoh
Outrage upon outrage

"Say to the king, my lord, Sun of all countries: Message of Rib-Hadda, your servant, footstool of your feet; ...

Is the activity of Abdi-Asirta, the dog, with the result that the lands of the king are joined to him, pleasing in the sight of the king, my lord, so he has **done nothing for his lands**?

Now indeed, Sumur, my lord's court and his bedchamber, has been joined to him. He has slept in the bed chamber of my lord, and opened the treasure room of my lord, and yet the king has done nothing. Who is he, the traitor and dog, that he is strong? ...

May my lord send men to take the possessions of my Adonis to the king my lord, lest that dog take the possessions of your god."

EA85

Gubal king Rib-Addi to Pharaoh
Nothing to eat

"Say to the king, my lord, the Sun: Message of Rib-Hadda, your servant, I fall at your feet 7 times and 7 times; ...

May the king, my lord heed the words of his loyal servant and may you send grain in ships in order to keep his servant and his city alive. **May he grant 400 men and 30 pairs of horses** as were given to Surata, that they may guard the city for you. ...

Listen to me. Tell Yanhamu to take the money for the people of Gubla in the land of Yarimuta. Moreover the king of Mittana came out as far as Sumur, and though wanting to march as far as Gubla, he returned to his own land, as there was no water for him to drink. **I keep writing like this to the palace** for what I need. **Why do you not reply**, "What my servant requests is available, or is not available", so I may know what I should do until the king arrives and visits his loyal servant?"

EA86

Gubal king Rib-Addi to Amanappa
Complaint via an official

... "Listen to me! The war is severe, so **come with archers** that you may take the land of Amurru. **Day and night it has cried to you** and they say that what is taken from them to Mitanna is very much. So now are you yourself must not say, " Why should I come out". ... or send ships so I myself can get out."

EA87

Gubal king Rib-Addi to Amanappa
Broken promises

... "Why did **you lead me astray**, saying, "Send your messenger here to me before the king so he may give you troops and chariots as a help so you can take the city? So I listened to your words, and I sent him, and **he came out empty-handed**. Then I heard that there were **no troops with him**, and as a result Batruna was joined to him.""

EA88

Gubal king Rib-Addi to Pharaoh
Blockaded

... "I have written repeatedly to you, "The war is against Ardat, against Irqat, and against ... Ammiya and Sigata, loyal cities of the king, but the **king, my lord, has done nothing**. Moreover, what is he, Abdi-Asirta, the servant and dog, that he has acted as he pleased in the lands of my lord, and yet the king, my lord, has done nothing for his servant? ..."

EA89

Gubal king Rib-Addi to Pharaoh
The need in Tyre

... "**Though I keep writing like this to the palace**, my words are not taken to heart, and they go **utterly unheeded**. Look at the deed in Tyre. On this account I am afraid. Even now the king makes no enquiry about his mayor, my brother. May the king heed my words ... I assure you, they have killed their mayor together with my sister and her sons. ... He wrote again and again to the king, but his words went unheeded, and so he died. I know it! ... May the king terrify them! Do I not continue to write of their crime to the king?"

EA90

Gubal king Rib-Addi to Pharaoh
Alone and unheeded

... "Be informed that the war against me is severe. He has taken all my cities; Gubla alone remains to me. I was in Sigata and I wrote to you, "Give thought to your city lest Abdi-Asirta take it. But **you did not listen to me. My words went unheeded**, and they were not taken to heart. **You yourself have been negligent of your cities** so that the Apiru dog takes them. It is to you that I have turned... Day and night everyone **awaits the coming forth of archers**. I have been plundered of my grain and it is to you that I have turned ."

EA91

Gubal king Rib-Addi to Pharaoh
A plea

... "Why have you **sat idly by and done nothing**, so that the Apiru dog takes your cities? When he took Sumur I wrote to you, "Why do you do nothing?" Then it was taken. When he saw that there was no one that said anything to him about Sumur, his intentions were reinforced, so that he strives to take Gubla. ... **May you pay 1000 shekels of silver and 100 shekels of gold so he will go away from me**. What can I do by myself? I go on **writing like this for archers and an auxiliary force**, but my words go unheeded. Moreover, give thought yourself to your lands. Moreover, listen to me and if there are no archers and auxiliary force then there will be no ... for Gubla and it will be joined to the Apiru."

EA92

Gubal king Rib-Addi to Pharaoh
Some help from the Pharoah

... "So what am I to do? I sent my messenger to the king, my lord, in regard to my city is that Abdi-Asirta has taken. Abdi-Asirta heard that my man had arrived from the king, my lord, and he heard that there was nothing with him. Since **there was no auxiliary force that came out to me**, he has now moved up against me. And what could I say? Moreover it was a gracious deed of my king, my lord, that the king wrote to the king of Beirut, to the king of Sidon, and to the king of Tyre, saying, 'Rib-Hadda will be writing to you for an auxiliary force, and all of you are to go.' ... May it seem right in the sight of the king my lord that they should send soldiers of an expeditionary force."

EA93

Gubal king Rib-Addi to Amanappa
An angry vassal

... "Look, I was distressed, and angry at your words, 'I am on my way to you.' You are always writing like this to me! Listen to me. **Tell the king to give you 300 men** so we can visit the city and regain it for the king. Do not the **commissioners long for the coming out of the archers**? ... **Things are not as they were previously**."

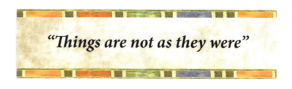

"Things are not as they were"

EA94

Gubla man to Pharaoh
Treachery everywhere

... "Why has my lord **not heeded** the word of his servant? My lord should know that there is no evil in the words of his servant. I do not speak any treacherous words to the king, my lord. The king, my lord, has examined the words and has heard the words! I said to the king, my lord, '**Send archers** to take Abdi-Asirta.' Treacherous men say treacherous things ..."

EA95

Gubal king Rib-Addi to chief
Men from Meluhha

... "May the king of Egypt send his commissioner that he may take it for him. Moreover, come yourself with all speed, and take everything. **Then return to get the archers** later on. Moreover, get... 200 men of Meluhha... Abdi-Asirta is very [ill?]..."

EA103

Gubal king Rib-Addi to Pharaoh
Critical days

... "My situation is very difficult. The war of the sons of Abdi-Asirta against me is severe. They have occupied the land of Amurru, and the entire country is theirs. Sumur and Irqata remain to the magnate. I have now been in Sumur because the magnate is in difficulty due to the war. ... The magnate keeps writing to them but they pay no attention to him. ... **If you do not send archers**, then there will not be a city remaining to you. But if archers are on hand, we will take all the lands for the king."

EA104

Gubal king Rib-Addi to Pharaoh
Ulassa taken

... "May the king, my lord, know that Pu-bahla, the son of Abdi-Asirta, has occupied Ulassa... All the cities are theirs. So may the king send an auxiliary force to Sumur until the king give thought to his land. ...

Previously, they would take cities of your mayors and you did nothing. Now they have driven out your commissioner and have taken his cities for themselves. If in these circumstances you do nothing, then they are certainly going to take Sumur and kill the commissioner and the auxiliary force in Sumur. What am I to do? ... an agreement has been made with the Apiru."

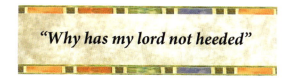

"Why has my lord not heeded"

EA105

Gubal king Rib-Addi to Pharaoh
Sumur under siege

… "Look at Sumur! Like a bird in a trap: so is Sumur: the sons of Abdi-Asirta by land, the people of Arwada by sea, are against it day and night. … Consider the case of the people of Arwada. **When the archers came out**, all the property of Abdi-Asirta in their possession was not taken away, and their ships by an agreement left Egypt. Accordingly, they are not afraid. Now they have taken Ulassa, and they strive to take Sumur. They have taken the army ships together with everything belonging to them, and I am unable to go to the aid of Sumur."

EA106

Gubal king Rib-Addi to Pharaoh
Sumur holding out

… "As for Sumur, the war against it is severe, and it is severe against me. Sumur is now raided up to the city gate. They have been able to raid it, but they have not been able to capture it. Moreover, 'Why does Rib-Hadda keep sending the tablets this way to the palace?' (because) he is more distraught than his brothers about Sumur. Look in my case there has been war against me for 5 years. Accordingly I keep writing to my lord. Look, I am not like Yapah-Hadda, and I am not like Zimredda. All brothers have deserted me. There is war against Sumur, and now its commissioner is dead. Indeed, I myself am now in distress. I was in Sumur, and all its people fled. …

May it seem right to my lord, **may he send 20 pairs of first class horses** to his servant; there are many men on my side; so that I can march against the enemies of the king, my Lord."

EA107

Gubal king Rib-Addi to Pharaoh
Charioteers but no horses

… "May the archer commander stay in Sumur, but fetch Haip to yourself, examine him, and find out about his affairs. Then if it pleases you, appoint as its Commissioner someone respected by the kings mayors. May my lord heed my words. Seeing that Aziru, the son of Abdi-Asirta, is in Damascus along with his brothers, send archers that they might take him, and the land of the king be at peace. If things go as they are now, Sumur will not stand. Moreover, may the *Amulet made of* king, my lord, heed the words of his loyal servant. There is no money to pay *electrum wire.*

for horses; everything is gone so that we might stay alive. So **give me 30 pairs of horses along with chariots**. I have charioteers but I do not have a horse to march against the enemies of king. Accordingly, I am afraid, and accordingly, I have not gone to Sumur."

EA108

Gubal king Rib-Addi to Pharaoh

Unheard-of deeds

… "Is it pleasing in the sight of the king, who is like Baal and Samas in the sky, that the sons of Abdi-Asirta do as they please? **They have taken the king's horses and chariots**, and they have sold into captivity charioteers and soldiers to the land of Subaru. In whose lifetime has such a deed been done? False words are now being spoken in the presence of the king, the Sun, I am your loyal servant, and whatever I know or have heard I write to the king, my lord. Who are they, the dogs, that they could resist the archers of the king, the Sun? **I wrote to your father and he heeded my words, and he sent archers**. Did he not take Abdi-Asirta for himself? …

Send me 20 men from Meluhha and 20 men from Egypt to guard the city for the king the Sun my lord. I am your loyal servant."

EA109

Gubal king Rib-Addi to Pharaoh

Then and now

… "In times past, whenever the king of Mittana was at war with your ancestors, your ancestors did not desert my ancestors. Now the sons of Abdi-Asirta, the servant and dog, have taken the cities of the king and the cities of his mayor, just as they please; they are the ones that took Ardata for themselves. **And you did nothing about their actions** when you heard of them.

For my part, I keep saying, 'If the king gives heed for a day, in that day the king will take them. And if he gives heed for a night, in that night he will take them. Accordingly, I am firm in my resolve. They have taken the treasures of your mayors, and they have taken the charioteers, your chariots, and soldiers, but you have done nothing. …

Previously, on seeing a man from Egypt, the kings of Canaan fled before him, but now the sons of Abdi-Asirta make men from Egypt prowl about like dogs. Death would be sweet to me. Let them not to be arrogant towards my Lord and my life. …"

EA110

Gubal king Rib-Addi to Pharaoh
The army's ships

… "No ship of the Army is to leave Canaan. **Why does he not give me** some of the royal property that the ships of the army transport, and then the mayors …"

EA111

Gubal king Rib-Addi to Pharaoh
Army activity

… "If this year **there are no archers**, then all lands will be joined to the Apiru. Look, members of the army have entered Akka in order to transport…"

EA112

Gubal king Rib-Addi to Pharaoh
Questions for the king

… "Why does the king, my lord, write to me, 'Guard! Be on your guard!' With what shall I guard? With my enemies, or with my peasantry? Who would guard me? If the king guards his servant, then I will survive. But if the king does not guard me, who will guard me? If the king sends men from Egypt and Meluhha, and horses in the charge of this man of mine, with all speed, then I will survive to serve the king, my lord. …

If the king wants his servant and his city to survive, then **send a garrison to guard your city** and your settlement until the king is really concerned for his lands, sends his archers, and brings peace to his lands. …"

EA113

Gubal king Rib-Addi to Egypt official
War and peace

… "He has plundered 2 of my ships and my sheep and goats so that the amount of my property in his possession is very large, **may the king send his commissioner** to decide between the two of us. Everything that is taken from him may the king take. Concerning my property that is in his possession he should enquire of my men; from Rib-Hadda and for the Apiru even has all of it been acquired. …"

EA114

Gubal king Rib-Addi to Pharaoh
Loyalty & its rewards

... "May the king give thoughts to his city and his servant; my peasantry long only to desert. If you are unable to rescue me from my enemies then send back word so I can know what action I am to take. Look, I must keep writing like this to you about Sumur. Look, I did go and I strongly urged the troops to guard it, but now they have abandoned it, and the garrison has deserted. And for this reason I keep writing. I have sent a messenger of mine time and again. ...

Why are you negligent? The king **must send a garrison** to protect your loyal servant, ... Moreover, give thought to me. Who will be loyal were I to die? Look, Yapah-Hadda is on the side of Aziru."

EA116

Gubal king Rib-Addi to Pharaoh
Who do they think they are?

... "Note that I am your loyal servant, but I have nothing but distress. Note this matter. Note that I am the dirt at your feet, O king! Note: did not your father come out and visit his lands and his mayors? And now the gods and the Sun and the Lady of Gubla have granted that you be seated on the throne of your father's house to rule your land. Who are they, the sons of Abdi-Asirta, that they have taken the lands of the king for themselves? The king of Mitanni? The king of Kassu? The king of Hatti? **May the king send archers** and Yan-hamu along with the prefects from the land of Yarimuta."

EA117

Gubal king Rib-Addi to Pharaoh
A lesson from the past

... "The king, my lord, keeps saying, 'Why do you alone keep writing to me?' Here is my situation: there is not a mayor from Sumer that supports me, and indeed everyone is turned against me. And the 2 men from Egypt whom I sent to the palace have not come out. Did I not write to the king, 'There is no one to bring my tablet to the palace. It is these 2 men that must bring a tablet to the king.' And now, as they have not come out, I am accordingly afraid and I have turned to my lord.

Moreover, I sent a man to your father. When Amarnappa came with a small force, I wrote to the palace that **the king should send a large force**. ...

Previously, I would desire to send a man; ... I sent men to Egypt and a garrison was sent to me in their charge. Accordingly, I have sent this man. ...

If **the king does not want to send archers**, may he write to Yanhamu and Pihura, 'March along with your mayors. Take the land of Amurru'. In a day they will take it. ...

Look, in the days of my ancestors, there was property of the king at their disposal, and the garrison of the king was with them. But now, as for me, the war is severe against me. I have become afraid of my peasantry. Thus must **I be the one that keeps writing to the palace for a garrison** and men from Meluhha. But you have not written. ..."

EA118

Gubal king Rib-Addi to Pharaoh
Not like other mayors

... "that my only purpose is to serve the king in accordance with the practice of my ancestors, **may the king send archers** and pacify them. As for the mayors, since the cities are theirs and they are at peace, they do not keep writing to the king. ..."

EA119

Gubal king Rib-Addi to Pharaoh
Recalling past kindnesses

... "**I keep writing like this to the palace for a garrison and forces** in order that I may guard his city. What am I to do? While alive I shall guard the king's city for him, but if I die, what can I do?

As to its being said to the king, 'Rib-Hadda has caused the death of some royal archers', since the commissioners are alive, let me tell about all their deeds so the king will know that I am a loyal servant. ..."

EA121

Gubal king Rib-Addi to Pharaoh
Past and present

... "I wrote to the king, my lord, **'Send archers'**. Did they not take in a day the lands for the king, your father? Now, may the king heed the words of his servant and send archers to take the land of the king for the king... have they not been killed like dogs, and you have done nothing?"

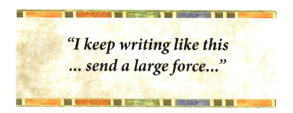

"I keep writing like this ... send a large force..."

EA122

Gubal king Rib-Addi to Pharaoh
An enormity

... "...consider that **previously, in the days of my ancestors, there was a garrison** of the king with them and property of the king was at their disposal, but as far as I am concerned, there are no provisions from the king at my disposal, and there is no garrison of the king with me.

I must guard myself by myself ... there is a garrison ... of the king with him, and there are provisions from the king at his disposal, but for me there is neither garrison nor provisions from the king. Pahura has committed an enormity against me. ...

I keep writing like this to the palace but my words are not heeded."

EA123

Gubal king Rib-Addi to Pharaoh
An enormity; another version

... "As to the king's writing, 'Guard yourself', with what am I to guard? Send the 3 men who Pihura brought in and then I will survive; Abdi-Rama, Yattin-Hadda, Abdi-Milki.

May the king send archers to take them."

EA124

Gubal king Rib-Addi to Pharaoh
The tireless correspondent

... "so may the king come out, as your ancestors did. The traitors have rebelled against the king. **Why has the king not sent charioteers and archers** to take the cities? If he is unable to take them, then he will also take Gubla from you. You will not take it ever again. If the king's desire is to guard his city, grant and send a garrison with all speed..."

EA125

Gubal king Rib-Addi to Pharaoh
A study in contrasts

... "As to **the king saying, 'Guard yourself...' with what shall I guard myself** and the city of the king? Previously, there was a garrison of the king with me, and the king was accustomed to give grain for their food from the land of Yarimuta. But now Aziru has repeatedly raided me. .."

EA126

Gubal king Rib-Addi to Pharaoh
Rejection of Byblos or Rib-Hadda?

... "Previously, money and everything for their provisions were sent from the palace to my ancestors, and my lord would send troops to them. But **now I write for troops, but a garrison is not sent, and is nothing at all is given** to me. As for the king, my lords, having said, "Guard yourself and the city of the king where you are", how am I to guard it?

I have indeed sent my messenger to the king, my lord, but troops are not sent, and my messenger you do not allow to come out. So send him along with rescue forces. ...

Why is nothing given to me from the palace? ... the Hittite troops and they have set fire to the country. I have written repeatedly, but no word comes back to me. ..."

EA127

Gubal king Rib-Addi to Pharaoh
Alone against the world

... "**May my lord grant 100 men and 100 soldiers** from Kasi, and 30 chariots, that I may guard the land of my lord **until a large force of archers** comes out..."

EA129

Gubal king Rib-Addi to Pharaoh
A review of the situation

... "Look, as to the king, my lords, having written to me, **'Troops have indeed come out', you spoke lies: there are no archers**; they do not come out. And they are stronger than we are. Look, unless archers come out within this year they will take Gubla. If Gubla is taken, then they will be strong. What will the troops do for your servant, Rib-Hadda? For my ancestor, earlier kings guarded Gubla, and you yourself must not abandon it.."

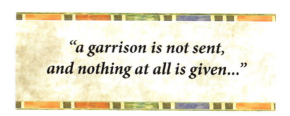

"a garrison is not sent, and nothing at all is given..."

EA130

Gubal king Rib-Addi to Pharaoh
Life among the Apiru

... "Look, formerly my ancestors were strong. There was a war against them, but a garrison of the king was with them. There were provisions from the king at their disposal. ...

What am I, who live among Apiru, to do? If now there are no provisions from the king for me, my peasantry is going to fight against me. All lands are at war against me. If the desire of the king is to guard his city and his servant, **send a garrison to guard the city**. I will guard it while I am alive. When I die, who is going to guard it?"

EA131

Gubal king Rib-Addi to Pharaoh
A commissioner killed

... "If the desire of the king, my lord, is to guard Gubla, then **may my lord send 300 soldiers, 30 chariots and 100 men from Kasi**, that they may guard Gubla, the city of my lord. If the king does not send the summer grain, should troops advance on Gubla, they will surely take it, and me, your servant, they will kill. They have attacked commissioners; counsellors of the king. When Pewuru, the king's counsellor, was killed, he was placed in...

EA132

Gubal king Rib-Addi to pharaoh 48
The hope for peace

... **"Send the royal archers**, and the entire land will be taken in a day. Did he not take for himself Abdi-Asirta, together with his possessions? Now Aziru has gathered all the Apiru and has said to them, if Gubla is not ...

I keep writing like this to the palace, but no attention is paid to me. Send ships to fetch the Lady's property and me. Send 50 to 100 men and 50 to 100 men from Meluhha, 50 chariots, to guard the city for you. Send archers and bring peace to the land."

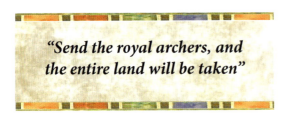

"Send the royal archers, and the entire land will be taken"

EA133

Gubal king Rib-Addi to Pharaoh
Some advice for the king

… "The sons of Abdi-Asirta have taken all your cities. They are at war with me. As Haip is with you, ask him. And may it seem right in your sight, **then send a garrison to your cities with all speed. I keep writing like this to the king**, my lord; send me 10 men from Meluhha that I may guard…"

EA134

Gubal king Rib-Addi to Pharaoh
Departure of the gods

"… From time immemorial the gods have not gone away from Gubla. Now Aziru has sent troops to seize it, so that we must give up our gods, and they have gone forth. And there being **no troops in the city** to smite the servant, the evil dog, they cannot return. What am I to do by myself? …

As I have sent a man of mine to the palace, why has the king not written? I wrote. Now the war against me is severe, and I am afraid."

EA136

Gubal king Rib-Addi to a Pharaoh
Rib-Hadda from Beirut

"… **I repeatedly wrote to the king, my lord, 'Send immediately a garrison** to your servant that they may guard the city for the king, my lord. No word, however from the king, my lord, has reached his servant. …

I am now awaiting day and night the archers of the king, my lord. May the king, my lord, give thoughts to his servant. If the king, my lord, does not have a change of heart, then I will die. May the king, my lord, give life to his servant. Moreover, they have given 2 of my sons and 2 of my wives to the rebel…"

EA137

Gubal king Rib-Addi to Pharaoh
An old man in exile

"… **I wrote repeatedly for a garrison, but it was not granted**, and the king, my lord did not heed the words of his servant. I sent a messenger of mine to the palace, but he returned empty-handed; he had no garrison. The men of my house saw that no money had been given, and so, like the mayors, my brothers, they did me injustice and despised me. …

I am old and there is serious illness in my body. The king, my lord, knows that the gods of Gubla are holy, and the pains are severe, for I committed sins against the gods. Accordingly, I shall not enter the presence of the king, my lord. So I herewith send my own son, a servant of the king, my lord, into the presence of the king. May the king heed the words of his servant, and may the king grant archers so they seize Gubla, and traitorous troops and the sons of Abdi-Asirti not enter it, and the archers of the king, my lord, be too few to take it. …"

EA138

Gubal king Rib-Addi to Pharaoh

From the depths

"… I sent a tablet to the palace of the king. **Now [nothing] has come out to me since 4 months** ago. Thus does my lord … for his servant. I am a servant of the king. The king has no royal mayor like me who will die for my lord. When Abdi-Asirta seized Sumur, I guarded the city by myself. There was no garrison with me, and so I wrote to the king my lord. …

So I wrote to the palace for troops, but no troops were given to me. Then the city said, 'Abandon him. Let's join Aziru!' I said, 'How could I join him and abandon the king, my lord? …

Previously I would write to the king; he would not heed my word. Now I am living in Beirut like a dog, and my word is still unheeded. If the king listened to his servant and troops were given to me, the city would return to the king, so may the king give troops that we may seize the city. …

Look, the people of Gubla keep writing, 'Where are the days when the king, your lord, used to write to you? **Where are the troops of the days when they were sent to you?**' … **Why has my lord neglected me?**"

EA139

Ilirabih Gubla to Pharaoh

A new voice, an old story

"… Do not **neglect** Gubla, your city and the city of your ancestors from most ancient times. Moreover, behold Gubla! Just has Hikupta, so is Gubla to the king, my lord. … Here is the crime that Aziru … against the king: he killed the king of Ammiya, and the king of Eldata, and the king of Irqata, and a commissioner of the king, my lord. He also broke into Sumur. …

So let him **send a garrison** to his city; 30 to 50 men, as far as Gubla. …"

EA140
The crimes of Aziru the Amorite

"... Moreover, why did the king communicate through Aziru? He does as he pleases. Aziru killed Aduna, the king of Irqata; he killed the king of Ammiya, the king of Ardata, and a magnate. He took their cities. ..."

EA141

Beirut king to Pharoah
Ammunira of Beirut gets a promise

"... Moreover, I have heard the words of the tablet of the king, my lord, my Sun, my god, the breath of my life, and the heart of your servant and the dirt at the feet of the king, my lord, my Sun and my god, the breath of my life, has rejoiced very, very much that the breath of the king, my lord, my Sun, my god, has come forth to his servant and the dirt at his feet.

Moreover, as to the king, my lord, my sons, having written to his servant and the dirt at his feet, **'Make preparations before the arrival of the archers** of the king, your lord,' I listened very, very carefully, **and I have indeed made preparations**, including my horses and my chariots and everything of mine that is available to the servant of the king, my lord, before the arrival of the archers of the king, my lord. And may the archers of the king, my lord, my Sun, my god, smash the heads of his enemies, and may the eyes of your servant look with pleasure on life from the king, my lord. ...

I will indeed guard of the city of the king **until I see the eyes of the archers** of the king, my lord..."

EA142

Beruta king Ammunira to Pharaoh
News about Byblos (Gubla)

"... I have heard the words of the tablet that the king, my lord, sent through Hani, and when I heard the words of the tablet of the king, my lord, my heart rejoiced and my eyes shone brightly. ...

Moreover I have indeed made preparations, including my horses and chariots and everything that is available to me, **before the arrival of the archers** of the king, my Lord."

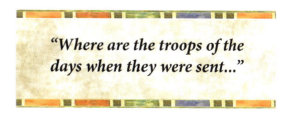

"Where are the troops of the days when they were sent..."

EA143

Beruta king Ammunira to Pharaoh
Egyptian ships in Beirut

"... Moreover, note how, as soon as ships of the king, my lord, that have been sailed into Beirut, come in, I release them.   ... **I am like a warmer of the horses** of the king, my lord..."

EA144

Zidon Zimriddi to Pharaoh
Zimreddi of Sidon gets a promise

"... When I heard the words of the king, my lord, when he wrote to his servant, then my heart rejoiced, and my head went high, and my eyes shone, at hearing the words of the king, my lord. ... May the king know that I have made preparations before the arrival of the archers of the king, my lord. I have prepared everything in accordance with the commander of the king, my lord.

May the king, my lord, know that the war against me is very severe. All the cities that the king put in my charge have been joined to the Apiru. May the king put me in the charge of a man that **will lead to the archers of the king** to call to account the cities that have been joined to the Apiru, so you can restore them to my charge that I may be able to serve the king, my lord, as our ancestors did before."

EA145

[Z]imrid[a] to an official
Word on Amurru

"... The king, and our lord, has indeed been earnestly addressed from his lands, but the **breath of his mouth does not reach** his servants..."

EA146

Tyre,_Lebanon to Pharoah
Abi-Milku of Tyre awaits word

"... You are the eternal Sun. The sweet breath of life belongs to my lord, my Sun, and I, your servant, am guarding Tyre, the city of the king, my lord, and waiting for the breath of the king. For me there is to be hostility **until the breath of the king comes to me with power.** .."

EA147

Tyre king AbiMilki to Pharaoh
A hymn to the Pharoah

"... The servant herewith writes to his lord that he heard the gracious messenger of the king who came to his servant, and the sweet breath that came forth from the mouth of the king, my lord, to his servant; his breath came back! Before the arrival of the messenger of the kingdom, my lord, **breath had not come back**; my nose was blocked. Now that the breath of the king has come forth to me I am very happy and satisfied, day by day. ...

When the king, my lord said, 'Prepare for the arrival of a large army,' then the servant said to his Lord, 'Yes yes yes!'. On my front and on my back I carry the word of the king, my lord. ... I am indeed to guarding Tyre, the principal city, for the king, my lord until the powerful arm of the king comes forth over me, to give me water to drink and wood to warm myself. ..."

EA148

Tyre king AbiMilki to Pharaoh
The need for mainland Tyre

"... The king, my lord, has written for glass. I give to the king, my lord, what I have on hand; 100 units in weight. May the king, my lord, give his attention to his servant and give Usu to his servant so he can drink a jug of water. **May the king, my lord, give 10 palace attendants to guard** his city in order that I may enter and see the face of my king. ..."

EA149

Tyre king AbiMilki to Pharaoh
Neither water nor wood

"... After I wrote an express tablet to the king, my lord, **he has not replied** to him. I am a commissioner of the kingdom, my lord, and I am one that brings good news and also bad news to the king, my lord. May the king send a palace attendant to guard his city in order that I may go into the king, my lord, to see his face. What is the life of a palace attendant when breath does not come forth from the mouth of the king, his lord? But he lives if the king writes to his servant, and he lives forever. ...

I sent a tablet to the king, my lord, but **he has not replied** to his servant. Since last year there has been war against me. There is no water, there is no wood. May he send a tablet to his servant so that he may go in and see his face. May the king give thought to his servant and to his city, and **may he not abandon his city** and his land. Why should a commissioner of the king, the lord, move away from the land? Zimredda knows, and the traitor knows, that the **arm of**

the king is absent. Now a palace attendant is bringing my tablets to the king, the Sun, my lord; may the king reply to his servant."

EA150

Tyre king AbiMilki to Pharaoh
Needed; just one soldier

".. Should **a single soldier guard** the city of the king, my lord then I would go in to behold the face of the king. May the king give his attention to his servant and give him Usu that he may live and drink water. They are wailing in the street that I should give them wood…"

EA151

Tyre king AbiMilki to Pharaoh
A report on Canaan

"… May the king, my **lord, not abandon** his servant. May the king, my lord, give his attention and give water for our drink and wood to his servant. …

The king, my lord wrote to me, 'Write to me what you have heard in Canaan' …"

EA152

Tyre king AbiMilki to Pharaoh
A demand for recognition

"… May the king, my lord, my god, my Sun, take cognizance of his city. **May he give me 10 soldiers to guard** his city, for the war against me is severe."

EA153

Tyre king AbiMilki to Pharaoh
Ships on hold

" … The entire land is afraid of the troops of the king, my lord. I have had my men to hold ships at the disposition of the troops of the king of my lord. …"

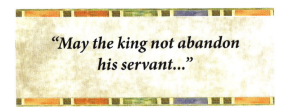

"May the king not abandon his servant…"

EA154

Tyre king AbiMilki to Pharaoh
Orders carried out

"… I have heard what the king wrote to his servant, 'Let my forces be prepared against Yawa,' What the king ordered, that I have carried out with the greatest joy. Moreover, since the departure of the troops of the king, my lord, from me, the ruler of Sidon does not allow me or my people to go to land to fetch wood or to fetch water for drinking."

EA155

Tyre king AbiMilki to Pharaoh
For the king's daughter Mayati?

"… Moreover, my lord, since the **departure of the troops** from me, I cannot go to land. Should a tablet of the king, my lord, arrive, then I will approach the land."

EA156

Amurru (Amorite) kingdom Aziri to Pharoah
From Aziru, a plea

"To the king, my lord, my god, my Sun: Message of Aziru, your servant. I fall at the feet of my lord 7 times and 7 times. …"

EA157

Amurru king Aziri to Pharaoh
Eager to serve

"… if the king of Hatti advances for war against me, the king, my **lord, should give me troops and chariots** to help me, and I will guard the land of the king, my lord. Moreover in all haste to send me my messenger, and I will …"

EA166

Amurru king Aziri to Haay
Coming- but not yet

"To Haay, my brother: Message of Aziru, your brother. For you may all go well, and for the archers of the king, my lord, may all go very well. …"

EA169

Amurru son of Aziri to an Egypt official

Aziru in Egypt

"In me there is no duplicity ... you may keep me alive and you may put me to death. ...

... I am repeatedly informed, 'Your father is staying in Egypt, and so we are going to wage war against you. .. Now indeed everyone is deserting."

EA171

Amurru son of Aziri to Pharaoh

Eager to serve

"... and now O king, my lord, Pawuru, the archer-commander of the king, has reached me. Pawuru knows my loyalty and may the Sun, the king, inquire from him..."

EA174

Bieri of Hasabu to Pharoah

"... **may the king give archers** that we may regain the cities..."

EA175

Ildayyi of Hasi to Pharoah

"... may the **king give archers** that we may regain the cities..."

EA176

Abdi-Risa to Pharoah

"... may the **king give archers** that we may regain the cities..."

Many of these later letters are very fragmented, but are thought to also be pleas for an army to be sent.

EA177

Yamiuta of Guddasuna to Pharoah

"... may the king ..."

EA180

... to Pharoah

"... **may the king send chariots** along with my son, that they may guard the cities..."

EA181

... to Pharoah

"... may the king send ... that they may guard the cities..."

EA182

Shuttarna_II of Musihuna to Pharoah

"... may **the king send a garrison**, that they may hold the cities..."

EA189

Qadesh mayor Etakkama to Pharoah
Apiru beaten at Kadesh

"... Since Biryawaza had allowed all of the cities of the king, muy lord, to go over to the Apiru in Tahsi and Upu, I went, and with your gods and your Sun leading me, I restored from the Apiru the cities to the king, my lord, for his service, and I disbanded the Apiru. May the king rejoice at Etakkama his servant..."

EA191

Arzawaija of Ruhiza to Pharoah

"... The king... wrote to me to make preparations before the arrival of the archers of the king, and before the arrival of his many commissioners. ..."

EA192

Ruhiza king Arzawaija to Pharoah

"... my **king must not neglect** his country. ..."

"May the king send chariots"

EA193

Dijate to Pharoah

"... **when the archers** come forth, I will accompany them. ..."

EA195

Damascus mayor Biryawaza to Pharoah
My Apiru?

"... I am indeed together with my troops and chariots, together with my brothers, my Apiru and my Suteans, at the disposition of the archers, wheresoever the king, my lord, shall order me to go."

EA196

Damascus mayor Biryawaza to Pharoah
Unheard-of deeds

"... **May a large force of the king, my lord, come immediately** against the king of Hatti. The garrison of the king, my lord, has left me. I am the servant of the king that has opened the way for the troops, but the king, my lord, should know that all the servants of the king have run off to Hatti, and all the commissioners of the king, my lord, who came forth. ...

No-one has ever done such a thing. Moreover may the king, my lord, send me 200 men to guard the cities of the king until I see the archers of the king, my lord."

EA197

Damascus mayor Biryawaza to Pharoah
Gave it to the Apiru!

"... Arsawuya went to Kissa and took some of Aziru's troops, and captured Sadu. He gave it to the Apiru and did not give it to the king, my lord. May the king look carefully to his land lest the enemies take it. May the king indeed be at one with his servant. May the **king not abandon** his servant, ..."

"May a large force come"

EA201

Artamanya to Pharoah
Ready for marching orders

"... as you have written me to make preparations before the arrival of the archers, who am I, a mere dog, that I should not go? I am here with, along with my troops and my chariots, at the disposition of the archers where ever the king, my lord, orders me to go."

EA202

Amajase to Pharoah
Ready for marching orders

"...who am I, a mere dog, that I should not go? I am herewith, along with my troops and my chariots, at the disposition of the archers where ever the king, my lord, orders me to go."

EA203

Abdi-Milki to Pharoah
Ready also for marching orders

"...Abdi-Milki ruler of Sashimi ,   ... I am herewith, along with my troops and my chariots, at the disposition of the archers where ever the king, my lord, orders me to go."

EA204

Qanu to Pharoah
Ready also for marching orders

"... you have **written me to make preparations before the arrival of the archers**... I am herewith, along with my troops and my chariots, at the disposition of the archers where ever the king, my lord, orders me to go."

EA205

Gubbu prince to Pharoah
Ready also for marching orders

"... You have written me to make preparations before the arrival of the archers... I am herewith, along with my troops and my chariots, at the disposition of the archers where ever the king, my lord, orders me to go."

EA206

Naziba to Pharoah
Ready also for marching orders

"… You have written me to make preparations before the arrival of the archers… I am herewith, along with my troops and my chariots, at the disposition of the archers where ever the king, my lord, orders me to go."

EA207

Ipteh to Pharoah
Lost to the Apiru

"… **Lost to the Apiru** from my control are all the cities of the king."

EA213

Zitrijara to Pharoah 3
Preparations

"… I have heard the message of the king, my lord, my Sun, my god, to his servant. I herewith make the preparations in accordance with the command of the king, my Lord, my son, my god.."

EA215

Baiawa to Pharoah
A warning

"… should Yanhamu not be here within this year, **all the lands are lost** to the Apiru. So give life to your lands."

EA216

Baiawa to Pharoah
Obedience to the commissioner

"… I have heard the message of the king, my lord, to his servant to make preparations before the arrival of the archers. I am now making preparations in accordance with the command of the king. I obey most carefully to the words of Maya, the commissioner of the king, my lord. **May the king, my lord, send archers** to his servants."

EA217

A[h]... to Pharoah
Maya the commissioner

"... May the king, **my lord, send troops** to his country, so that I can guard. The men who have not obeyed Maya, they shall ... all of them."

EA218

... to Pharoah
Preparations

"...May the king, **my lord, send troops** to his countries."

EA220

Nukurtuwa [Z]unu to Pharoah
Awaiting the commissioner

"... until the arrival of the commissioner of the king, my lord. May the king, my lord..."

EA227

Hazor (Hasuru) king
A happy king

"... Look, I have the cities of the king, my lord, under guard until my lord reaches me. And when I heard these words of yours and the coming forth of the Sun to me, I rejoiced accordingly. I pondered the news, and my jubilation came forth. There was peace, and the gods themselves looked favourably on me. And I have indeed prepared everything **until the arrival of the king**, my lord for..."

EA230

Iama to Pharoah
An unusual message!

"... **if a soldier** of yours comes to me, then I guard him. And the cities where I am are all really guarded for you. Just ask your commissioner whether they are really guarded. May you know that all your cities are safe and sound."

"All the lands are lost"

EA231

... to Pharoah
Following orders

"... I have guarded the city according what the king my lord, my god my son, wrote..."

EA234

Acco (Akka) king Satatna to Pharaoh
Like Magdalu in Egypt

" ... out came the troops of the king, my lord. He was with them in Magidda. Nothing was said to him. Then he deserted me, and Suta has just written to me..."

EA237

Bajadi to Pharoah
Under fire

"... May the king, my Lord, be informed that they have captured the cities of the king, my lord, but the city in which I am I now keep under guard **until I see** the eyes of the commissioner."

EA238

Bajadi to Pharoah
Absolute power

"... they have seized all the cities, and the city in which I am **I cannot guard**. So may the magnate, my lord, **send me a 50 man garrison to guard** the city until the arrival of the magnate, my lord."

EA243

Megiddo king Biridija to Pharaoh
Around the clock defense

"... and as the warring of the Apiru in the land is severe, **may the king, my lord, take cognizance** of his land..."

EA244

Megiddo king Biridija to Pharaoh
Beseiged by Labayu

"… May the king, my lord, know that **since the return to Egypt of the archers**, Labayu has waged war against me. We are thus unable to do the plucking. We are unable to go out of the city gate. When he **learned that archers were not coming out**, he immediately determined to take Magidda. Made a king save his city lest Labayu you seize it. **May the king give a garrison of 100 men** to guard his city lest Labayu seize it."

EA246

Megiddo king Biridija to Pharaoh
The sons of Labayu

"… The two sons of Labayu have indeed given their money to the Apiru and to the Suteans in order to wage war against me. May the king take cognizance of his servant."

EA251

… to Egypt official
Reckoning requested

"… let the king, my lord, demand of me a reckoning. **You have now in this way been negligent**. Surely the king, my lord, he is going to learn of this matter, and the king, my lord, will reply to me as he will, and the order of the king I will obey."

EA254

Labaya to Pharoah
Neither rebel nor delinquent

"… Moreover, the king wrote for my son. I did not know that my son was consorting with the Apiru. I herewith hand him over to Addaya. Moreover, how, if the king wrote for my wife, how could I hold her back?

How, if the king wrote to me, 'Put a bronze dagger into your heart and die,' how could I not execute the order of the king?"

EA263

... to lord
Robbed of everything

"... may my lord **send a garrison and horses**; my lord commanded his servant..."

EA269

Gezer mayor Milkili to Pharaoh
Archers and myrhh

"... I have heard what the king, my lord, wrote to me, and so may the king, my lord, **send the archers** to his servants, and may the king, my lord, send myrhh for medication."

EA270

Gezer mayor Milkili to Pharaoh
Extortion

"... May the king, my lord, know the deeds that he keeps doing to me since I left the king, my lord. **He indeed wants 2000 shekels of silver** from me, and he says to me, '**Hand over your wife and your sons** or I will kill you.' May the king know of this deed, and may the king my lord, **send chariots** and fetch me to himself lest I perish."

EA271

Gezer mayor Milkili to Pharaoh
The power of the Apiru

"... May the king, my lord, save his land from the power of the Apiru. Otherwise, may the king, my lord, **send chariots** to fetch us lest our servants kill us."

EA272

Sum[?] to Pharoah
Apiru activity

"... The entire land of the king, my lord, has **deserted to the Apiru**. May the king, my lord enquire of his commissioner about what is being done in the land of the king, so the king my lord will instruct his archers in my regard."

EA273

Ninurmahmes to Pharoah
From a queen mother

"... gone is the land of the king, my lord, by desertion to the Apiru. **May the king, my lord, take cognizance of his land**, and may the king, my lord, know that the Apiru wrote to Ayyaluna, and to Sarha and the 2 sons of Milkilu barely escaped being killed."

EA274

Ninurmahmes to Pharoah
Another city lost

"... May the king, my lord, save his land from the power of the Apiru lest it be lost. Sapuma has been taken. For the information of the king..."

EA279

Qiltu king Suwardata to Pharaoh
A wasteland

"... May the king, my lord, know that the land of the king is gone. I must drive back! I must go forth to Qeltu against the traitors. **May the king send archers**."

EA281

Qiltu king Suwardata to Pharaoh
A wasteland

"...May the king **send archers...**"

EA282

Qiltu king Suwardata to Pharaoh
Alone

"...May the **king send a very large archer force...**"

"*May the king take cognizance of his land... *"

EA283

Qiltu king Suwardata to Pharaoh
O to see the king

"If there are **still no archers** available, then may the king, my lord, take me away. ... May the kind send archers..."

EA284

Qiltu king Suwardata to Pharaoh
The powerful hand of the king

"...may the king, my lord, take me away. ... May the king send his powerful hand..."

EA285

Abdi-Hiba to Pharaoh
The soldier-ruler of Jerusalem

"... Message of Abdi-Heba your servant. I am not a mayor; I am a soldier for the king. Why has the king not sent a messenger? If **there are no archers available**, may the king send a commissioner that he may fetch the mayors to himself. And as for the garrison that belongs to Addaya, the commissioner of the king, I want their house. So may the king provide for them, may he send a messenger quickly."

EA286

Jerusalem king Abdi-Heba to Pharaoh
A throne granted, not inherited

"... and now O king, my lord, **there is no garrison**, and so may the king provide for his land. May the king provide for his land! All the lands of the king, my lord, have deserted. May he send a garrison so I may go in and visit the king, my lord. In truth, the king, my lord lives; whenever the commissioners come out I would say to them, 'Lost are the lands of the king', but they did not listen to me. Lost are all the mayors, there is not a mayor remaining to the king. The king has no lands. **The Apiru has plundered** all the lands of the king."

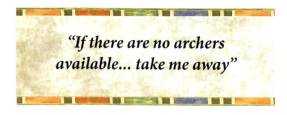

"If there are no archers available... take me away"

EA287

Jerusalem king Abdi-Heba to Pharaoh
A very serious crime

"... so may the **king provide for archers and send the archers** against men that commit crimes against the king, my lord. If this year there are archers in the lands then the mayors will belong to the king, my lord, but if there are no archers then the king will have neither lands nor mayors. Consider Jerusalem!"

EA288

Jerusalem king Abdi-Heba to Pharaoh
Benign neglect

"... now as the Apiru have taken the very cities of the king. Not a single mayor remains to the king, my lord; all are lost. **The king did nothing**. Why has he not called them to account? May the king provide for his land and **see to it that archers come out** to his land."

EA289

Jerusalem king Abdi-Heba to Pharaoh
A reckoning demanded

"... **May the king know that no garrison of the king is with me**. May the king send 50 men as a garrison to protect the land. The entire land of the king has deserted."

EA290

Jerusalem king Abdi-Heba to Pharaoh
Three against one

"... may the king give heed to Abdi-Heba, your servant, and **send archers to restore** the land of the king to the king. **If there are no archers**, the land of the king will desert to the Apiru."

EA298

Gezer mayor Iapahi to Pharaoh
A perfidious younger brother

"... May the king, my lord, be informed that my younger brother, having become my enemy, entered Muhhazu and has pledged himself to the Apiru."

EA299

Gezer mayor Iapahi to Pharaoh
A plea for help

"... since the Apiru are stronger then we, may the king, my lord, give me his help and may the king, my lord get me away from the Apiru lest the Apiru destroy us."

EA300

Gezer mayor Iapahi to Pharaoh
A servant like his father

"... **May they send his archers**. It is they alone who must get me back into my cities so I can serve the king, my lord in accordance with the practice of my father and his friends."

EA305

Subandu to Pharoah 5
Power of the Apiru

"... has the Apiru are more powerful than we are, **may the king take cognizance** of his lands.

EA318

Dagantakala to Pharoah
Save me!

"... **save me** from the powerful enemies, from the hand of the Apiru, Suteans and robbers. And save me, great king, my lord! And behold! I have written to you! Moreover, you great king, my lord, save me or I will be lost to the great king, my lord."

EA337

Hiziri to Pharoah
Abundant supplies ready... but no army yet

"... The king, my lord, wrote to me **prepare the supplies before the arrival of a large army of archers of the king**, my lord. May the god of the king, my lord, grant that the king, my lord come forth along with his large army and learn about his lands. I have in prepared accordingly abundant supplies before the arrival of a large army of the king."

EA362

Rib-Haddi to Pharoah

A commissioner murdered

"... **May the lord hasten the archers** or we must die. Because my lord has written to me, they know indeed that they are going to die, and so they seek to commit a crime."

EA366

Suwardata to Pharaoh

A rescue operation

"... may the king, my lord, be informed that the Apiru rose up against the lands, the god of the king, my lord, gave to me, and I smote him. And may the king, my lord, be informed that all my brothers have abandoned me. Only Abdi-Heba and I have been at war with that Apiru. Surata the ruler of Akka and Endaruta the ruler of Aksapa, these two also have come to my aid."

EA369

Egypt to ? in vassal state in Syria/Palestine; (probably never sent)

From the Pharoah to a vassal

"... to Milkilu, the ruler of Gazru; thus the king. **He herewith dispatches to you this tablet**, saying to you He herewith sends to you Hanya, the stable overseer of the archers, along with **everything for the acquisition of beautiful female cupbearers**: silver, gold, linen garments, carnelian, all sorts of precious stones, an ebony chair; all alike, fine things. Total value 160 diban. Total 40 female cupbearers; 40 shekels of silver being the price of a female cupbearer. Send extremely beautiful female cupbearers in whom there is no defect, so the king, your lord will say to you 'This is excellent, in accordance with the order he sent to you'. And know that the king is hale like the Sun. For his troops, his chariots, his horses, all goes very well. Amun has indeed put the upper land, and the lower land, where the sun rises, where the sun sets, under the feet of the king."

Foreign daughters and princesses were often given to Egyptian kings

There are many other fragments and letters similar to the above, most of them complaining in great detail about the sudden and sustained lack of Egyptian protective troops that had previously been active in Canaan.

NOT A 'PACIFIST'; JUST A MISSING ARMY

Surely the evidence now overwhelmingly points, not to Akhenaten being a 'pacifist', but rather his inheritance being a royal seat with no real military capability, at least for the first years of his reign.

There is nothing in his religious beliefs that seems to require the stance of pacifism; of course, his Egyptian homeland was not directly under threat, so his suggested pacifism was never challenged; nor did he even need to act in legitimate self-defence in a military way. For Egypt's own sake, there was no vital need to be the aggressor in Canaan either. He was far more interested in, maybe even stunned by, the homeland situation following the shocking, momentous failure of state religions and army, and the creation of a new world of truth, beauty, peace and the start of submission to a representation of this mysterious new powerful god that had truly taught his people a major lesson in godship, humility, real power and true sovereignty.

It takes years to train effective soldiers, especially archers. He did apparently use some Libyan mercenaries[2] although to what extent is not at all clear. He did evidently launch one military campaign against Nubia, the main source of gold, probably later in his reign. He also must have had a very small number of standing soldiers in Canaan or the Levant at the time of the Exodus; there is brief mention of this in some letters.

Akhenaten often seems to have especially promised 'archers', maybe playing for time as new ones were to be trained (although there is no evidence that this was ever achieved in his reign).

He also frequently arranged for the letter supplicants to arrange to guard each other, or themselves. How easy it would have been though, to send just a few of the hard men from the training camps at Memphis or Waset, if there were any. In many cases, this is all that was requested, as a deterrent, yet still denied.

There had been, at least under Amenhotep III's governance, garrisons at Gaza, Joppa, Sumur, Ulaza with its inland route to Ardata, strategic Beth Shean in the Jezreel Valley and Kumidu.

If Akhenaten had an army in the years immediately following the Exodus, you would think that he would have sent at least a small detachment of this world-beating army into the beleaguered Syrian arena, as the Hittites regained their strength and a timely strike, as fervently requested through the Amarna letters, would likely have been militarily beneficial to all. Even the sound or news of his dreaded archers, Nubian heavies and high-tech military, would have sent the Hittites scurrying back, like the effect of that fearsome sound of Scottish Highlanders Black Watch 'Ladies from Hell' in World War I.

Many of the Amarna letters desperately demand just such a detachment, recognizing the deterrent effect of even just a handful of crack troops sent at the right time. Those Egyptian archers appear to have had an SAS-like reputation in their day; the letters testify to this. If supported also by just a few simple, appropriate, government measures Akhenaten could easily have claimed a great victory not to mention the associated plunder and continued regional or global influence.

It is a matter of conjecture as to whether the tribute that had been pouring into Egypt since the glory days of Thutmose III, when that king's well-equipped army conquered a vast area reaching up beyond Byblos and Megiddo into Mitanni and Babylon, now started to dry up as the vassals and minor kings realized that Akhenaten was not honouring his part of the deal.

Interestingly also, the Egyptian army divisions were named after their old gods, so there would likely have been a lot of hollow-hearted and confused soldiers and charioteers as they raced after the Hebrews!

Their 'Arab' stallions, horses, and even many of their great leaders had come mostly from Asia; northern peoples we know as Aryan, Indo-European, and Semitic. Now, though, they were likely well settled in the great land of Egypt, and able to develop and produce these resources internally.

Akhenaten's attitude to the Canaanite pleaders, truly desperate as they evidently were, in their letters by the hundred, seems exceedingly cold-hearted. It appears that he was simply unable to muster any military support as had previously been expected and provided in abundance. He resorted to empty promises, even lies, playing for time in supporting his allies. He also was dealing with national shame, major disruption at home, and his own inexperience, youth, and a deeper interest in the arts. Was he a pacifist? There is actually no evidence of that persuasion in him.

Amarna had ceremonial, not military, horses

Also, on several wall reliefs there are depicted his royal chariot(s), with horses clearly harnessed and groomed for ceremonial purposes rather than military. These include the single relief fragment displayed in the Israel Museum, Jerusalem *(see photo on page 21)*, which is acknowledged there as featuring two parallel ceremonial horses with royal regalia, and pulling a royal chariot. Another famous depiction is a more comprehensive relief in the tomb of Merye where again it is clear that the setting is ceremonial. Also, the relief displayed in the Fitzwilliam Museum, Cambridge, is believed to be depicting foreign soldiers preparing for a royal parade. *(see photo on page 20),*

At the site of the 'window of appearance', where masses of the Amarna population would gather to receive royal hand-outs, there is shown to be a display of shields and spears, but there is no reason to believe that these were currently part of the hardware of an active military force.

There must have been an element of civil control or police presence, if only staffed by trainees. Also that a token reminder of potential military force may be displayed at times. It is hard to imagine how Akhenaten could have presented the knowledge of the loss of an entire army, but the populace must have known it as they retrieved the body of at least their Pharoah and probably hundreds, or thousands, of military bodies from the shores of the Red Sea.

In Summary

The Amarna Letters represent many hundreds of separate artefacts which, especially when taken together, prove:

(a) Egypt's army (referred to in the Letters as 'archers', 'chariots', 'garrisons', 'men', 'troops') is desperately demanded by the minor kings of Canaan, with virtually no response from Akhenaten despite many desperate situations and an earlier continuous military presence in that land, under the reign of Amenhotep III. Virtually all personnel of the army must have drowned in the Red Sea, as the *Bible* says, thus giving the modern impression that Akhenaten was a 'pacifist'.

(b) Egypt's gold ceased to be given to the kings of Canaan at this time, despite urgent pleas and a long history of gold generosity under the previous king; most of the available gold had evidently been given to the Israelites as they left Egypt, as the *Bible* says (*'they stripped the Egyptians'*, Exodus 12:36). Prior to Akhenaten's reign, Amenhotep III's gifts and supplies of gold had been amazingly abundant, in addition to his government managing the international scene with skill and good oversight of the troops, resources, and personnel.

(c) The tragic death of the previous king, Amenhotep III. The *Bible* says that Pharoah died with his troops (Psalm 136:10-16):

> *["Give thanks] to the One striking down Egypt in their firstborn ones: His steadfast love is eternal; and the One bringing Israel out from the midst of them: His steadfast love is eternal; with a strong hand and outstretched arm, His steadfast love is eternal; Who split apart the Red Sea, His steadfast love is eternal; and made Israel pass through it, His steadfast love is eternal; Who hurled Pharoah and his army into the Red Sea, His steadfast love is eternal; Who led His people through the wilderness."*

(d) Together, the Amarna Letters reveal the Exodus 'Pharoah' to be Amenhotep III, by showing the remarkable, sudden, unique and unannounced inability of his successor Akhenaten to raise an army or supplies of gold as had always previously been abundant.

Chapter 3

THE EXODUS

The Bible is the best source of information

The Hebrew account of powerful rescue,
a 40-year wandering, their likely route,
and arrival in Canaan

Life in Egypt after the Exodus

EXODUS

1 These are the names of the sons of Israel who came to Egypt with Jacob, each coming with his household: ²Reuben, Simeon, Levi, and Judah; ³Issachar, Zebulun, and Benjamin; ⁴Dan and Naphtali, Gad and Asher. ⁵The total number of persons that were of Jacob's issue came to seventy, Joseph being already in Egypt. ⁶Joseph died, and all his brothers, and all that generation. ⁷But the Israelites were fertile and prolific; they multiplied and increased very greatly, so that the land was filled with them.

⁸A new king arose over Egypt who did not know Joseph. ⁹And he said to his people, "Look, the Israelite people are much too numerous for us. ¹⁰Let us deal shrewdly with them, so that they may not increase; otherwise in the event of war they may join our enemies in fighting against us and rise from the ground."-a ¹¹So they set taskmasters over them to oppress them with forced labor; and they built garrison citiesᵇ for Pharaoh: Pithom and Raamses. ¹²But the more they were oppressed, the more they increased and spread out, so that the [Egyptians] came to dread the Israelites.

¹³The Egyptians ruthlessly imposed upon the Israelites ¹⁴ᶜ-the various labors that they made them perform. Ruthlessly-ᶜ they made life bitter for them with harsh labor at mortar and bricks and with all sorts of tasks in the field.

¹⁵The king of Egypt spoke to the Hebrew midwives, one of whom was named Shiphrah and the other Puah, ¹⁶saying, "When you deliver the Hebrew women, look at the birthstool: ... ¹⁷The

The Bible as reliable history:

Yves Bonnefoy, in the great 2-volume work
Mythologies, Vol.1 p184, says:

"[The Bible] constitutes a mine of information about all aspects of the West Semitic religions, including those foreign to the religion of Israel. This mine has still been exploited only sporadically and somewhat tendentiously, that is to say solely or almost solely from a biased point of view."

What the Bible says about the Exodus

THERE FOLLOWS here a concise précis of the Hebrew Bible account. (See especially the *Tanakh* version of the Exodus, published by *The Jewish Publication Society*; and the *Interlinear Hebrew-English Old Testament*, Kohlenberger, published by Regency Reference Library).

[Genesis 15:7] "I am Yahweh who brought you (Abram) out from Ur, to assign you this land as your possession."

God's promise to Abram for the Promised Land, a unique land of topographical extremes.

[Genesis 22:17] "I shall surely bless you ... and your seed... your seed will take possession of the gate of your foes."'

Exodus 1: 6 "Eventually Joseph died, and also all his brothers and all that generation. And the sons of Israel became fruitful and multiplied, becoming exceedingly numerous, so that the land became filled with them. In time there arose a new king who did not know Joseph.

Note that Joseph belongs to an earlier generation, well before the Exodus.

1:13 the Egyptians made the sons of Israel slave under oppression. They kept making their life bitter with hard slavery at mortar and bricks ... and every form of slavery.

1:15 king of Egypt said to the Hebrew midwives ... if it is a son, you must kill it ... however the midwives feared the true God and they did not ...

This new Pharoah is likely to have been Amenhotep III, who reigned for 38 years.Exhibits of actual bricks from this period can be seen in the Met Art Museum, New York also the British Museum.

1:22 Pharoah commanded all his people ... cast every newborn son into the River Nile ...

2:1-10 Levi ... woman became pregnant ... concealed in ark of bulrushes ... his sister kept watch ... Pharoah's daughter came to bathe with her female handmaids ... she felt compassion ... 'this is one of the Hebrews' ... 'call a Hebrew nurse' ... he became a son to Pharoah's daughter ... called him Moses

Moses was raised within the innermost chambers of the royal household; his spiritual influence must have been felt by most of the royals. They evidently knew he was a Hebrew, from the start.

3:2-8 "(to Moses, with the sign of the burning bush) I have seen the affliction of my people in Egypt; I have heard their outcry; I am going to deliver them out of the hand of the Egyptians to bring them to a land flowing with milk and honey, to the land of the Canaanites..."

Exodus 23:28-30 indicates God's intention to gradually drive out the Canaanite tribes from the 'Promised Land', rather than kill them.'

3:15-20 "God said, 'This is what you must say to Pharoah, 'Yahweh[1] has sent me to you ... this is my name forever ... I shall strike Egypt with my wonderful acts'."

The Name of God is featured prominently in these chapters; a Name provided by Himself, with a very powerful meaning.[1]

5:16 no straw is given to the servants; they must gather their own straw and make bricks, and are beaten also

6:7 "I shall indeed take you to me as a people, and I shall prove to be God to you."

7:7 Moses was 80 years old and Aaron was 83 when they spoke to Pharoah.

7:19 (Plague 1: Nile becomes blood) for 7 days.

8:2 (Plague 2: frogs everywhere)

8:16 (Plague 3: gnats everywhere)

8:21 (Plague 4: gadflies in all the land) Egypt priests acknowledge 'it is the finger of God!'

9:3-7 (Plague 5: pestilence on the field animals of the Egyptians only) Pharoah sees the distinction.

9:8 (Plague 6: boils and blisters on Egypt's men and beasts)

9:16 God taunts Pharoah 'for the sake of showing you my name and power' ... are you still haughty?

9:18-21 (Plague 7: hail and rain only on selected Egyptian stock)

10:4 (Plague 8: locusts strip the shrubs and vegetation)

10:22 (Plague 9: dense darkness in Egyptian areas and homes for three days)

11:4 (Plague 10: death of [male] firstborn except those with blood on lintels ['passover'])

12:2 [New Jewish calendar started] [Passover instructions given; blood, hyssop, lamb, unfermented cakes and bitter greens]

12:12 "against all the gods of Egypt I shall execute judgements. I am Yahweh."

12:29-36 firstborn are struck ... a great outcry among the Egyptians ... 'send them away in haste as we are all dead men' ... they stripped the Egyptians (of gold, silver and clothing)

12:40 Israel had lived in Egypt and Canaan for 430 years; it came about at the end of the 430 years, on the very day. ... this day is for observance throughout the generations.

It is possible to calculate exactly the time of the Exodus, by assembling the various periods stated precisely in Scripture . See Chapter 7 in this book.

See Chapter 5 in this book for a discussion on how each plague related to the shaming of Egypt's gods.

Most of the Israelites evidently lived in the north of Egypt, although many will have been enslaved in households throughout the land. Almost all of the plagues did not affect the Israelites.

Hyssop is a symbol of humility.

The wine of later Passovers is a symbol of the blood used at this time, to mark the door lintels.

See the Amarna Letters for many references to the lack of Egypt gold in years following the Exodus.

Abraham crossed the Euphrates into his land of promise in 1943 BCE, according to Bible chronology.

12:48 [circumcision begins]

13:3 "Remember this day ... mighty hand freed you"

13:17 "God did not lead them by the way of the Philistines lest they get afraid and turn back ... he led them via the wilderness and the Red Sea, in battle formation."

This is the start of the Israelite nation as a unified religious tribe. Before this, they were a devout family who had prayed to YHWH as their 'Most High' God, as at Genesis 14:22

13:19 Moses was taking Joseph's bones with him ... they went via Succoth and Etham at the edge of the wilderness.

13:21-22 "Yahweh went ahead of them in a pillar of cloud by day and a pillar of fire by night"

14:2-4 route turns back via Pihahiroth, Migdol, Baalzephon. Pharoah chases, thinking Israelites are confused and lost.

The route taken by the Israelites is reasonably precise in the account.

14:6 Pharoah made 600 best war chariots and all the others ready together with his warriors and he took his people with him.

We read that Pharoah brought together virtually all of his combined forces, and suffered a total loss.

14:20-21 the night was lit up showing a light-bearing cloud on one side and intense darkness on the other ... the sea is parted.

14:23-25 Pharoah's army chases into sea after the Israelites; the wheels come off the chariots; the Egyptians begin to say 'Yahweh certainly fights against us'

14:28 "not one of them remained" [Psalm 136:15]

Pharoah dies; see also Psalm 106:11, "not one of them was left."

15:1-21 [victory song]

12: 37 "and a vast mixed company also went up with them, as well as flocks and herds."

32: 4 Aaron supervises the making of a solid gold calf

[Deut 2:14] "that whole generation of men of war perished from the camp (of Israel)."

Huge amount of gold used to make a gold calf, also later a large tabernacle made of huge quantities of gold and silver, along with altar utensils.

[Numbers 14:34] the Israelites wander for 40 years.

[Numbers 21:3] The Israelites conquer Canaan (but fail to subdue the entire land).

'men of war'; see Chapter 8 of this book regarding the 'Hapiru' (Apiru).

[1 Kings 6:1] Solomon's temple began to be built 480 years after the Exodus (in Solomon's 4th year of reign).

[Psalm 105:27-44] Summary of Exodus and gradual settling of inheritance.

Life in Egypt after the Exodus

The Egyptian army is likely to have been comprised of some of the top men of Egypt; nobles and local masters, as it was in the Crusades and in other armies throughout history. If this was the case, when the army was destroyed in the Red Sea there would have been a vacuum in authority over the homes of the wealthy when it was realised that these men would not be returning; this seems to be suggested by similar descriptions in the *Ipuwer Papyrus* [2] (now in Leiden Museum, Netherlands) relating probably to an earlier crisis.

The described prevalence of disease may help explain the rapidity with which the site of Akhet was subsequently abandoned. It may also explain why later generations considered the gods to have turned against the Amarna monarchs. Arielle Kozloff [3] discusses the evidence for this, arguing that the epidemic was caused by Bubonic plague over polio.

The *Ipuwer Papyrus* [2] is generally viewed as hypothetical 'admonitions', and is apparently from an earlier period than the commonly accepted Exodus date, judging by its grammar, but it helps one to visualise the anarchy that may have been in Egypt after the Exodus killed off the Pharoah, all the male firstborn and all authority of the priests, gods and kingship, not to mention many of its nobles and possibly other social support systems and personnel.

It is thought to be a re-write of an earlier (12th Dynasty?) similar text, maybe based on similar devastation. Even if the *Papyrus* is not actually from that period, it helps to show what life may well have been like:

> *"[What Ipuwer said when he addressed the Majesty of the Lord of All ... an empty waste ... a man goes to plough with his shield ... The virtuous man goes in mourning because of what has happened in the land ... No one is left to maintain order ... pestilence is throughout the land, blood is everywhere ... many dead are buried in the river; the stream is a sepulcher ... men are few ... barbarians from abroad have come to Egypt ... there are no Egyptians anywhere ... without paying taxes owing to civil strife ... he who was buried as a falcon [a dead king] is devoid of biers ...*
>
> *If I knew where God is, then I would serve Him."... the children of princes are dashed against walls ... the private council-chamber, its writings are taken away and the mysteries which were [in it] are laid bare ... Indeed, magic spells are divulged; smw- and shnw-spells are frustrated because they are remembered by men ... the poor man has attained to the state of the Nine Gods, and the erstwhile procedure of the House of the Thirty is divulged ... the secrets of the embalmers are thrown down ... men have fallen into rebellion against the Uraeus ... Re, even she who makes the Two Lands content ... no craftsmen work, for the enemies of the land have impoverished its craftsmen ... Lower Egypt weeps; the king's storehouse is the common property of everyone ...Where is he [the supreme god] today? Is he asleep? Behold, his power is not seen ...The troops whom we marshalled for ourselves have turned into foreigners and have taken to ravaging..."*

The date for the *Papyrus* is not certain. Toby Wilkinson[4] dated the papyrus to around the end of the Middle Kingdom (c1600 BCE). Most scholars have agreed to this approximate dating. It has textual characteristics that seem to have both Middle and Late dynastic qualities; the original may have been written earlier in the millennium and a redacted copy in the Late dynastic period, which would also explain the mixed style. There are also many gaps and misspellings in its text.

What would any new king do in this situation? He needs to restore order with a new credible authority that sees everything and acts fast; he has no real army but has to put a civil defence in place; the priests with their spells and gods are discredited and clearly not respected; there has been a great deal of death and now much unemployment and anarchy; most of Egypt appears to have had a radical change in population, with millions leaving the country, together with huge flocks, herds, and most of the country's valuables!

We can only imagine what it must have been like; whichever way you look at it, and whatever beliefs you have about Akhenaten or the Exodus, there were most certainly some unprecedented upheavals throughout the land at that time. No wonder there is little said about it in the records.

One fascinating inscription, described in more detail in Chapter 7 of this book, is 'Stela X', one of the boundary inscriptions at Amarna. It reads (with many gaps) in part, "... *effecting the expulsion of some of the people with the army in its entire ... and arranged ... at the beginning of ...*"

Also King 'Tut' after the 16 years of Akhenaten's reign, describes the huge loss of temples and old religious paraphanalia which the populace, and himself, wish to restore and rebuild.

Fragment of the
Ipuwer Papyrus

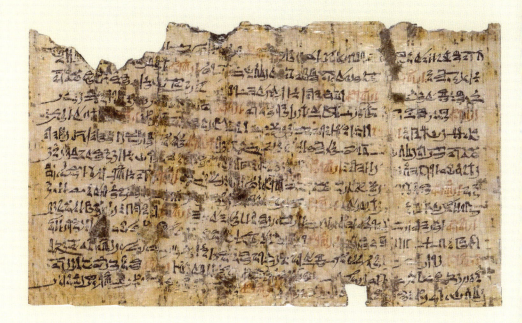

Top:

Statue of Amenhotep III as the centre-piece in the main lobby of the Metropolitan Art Museum, New York.

Bottom:

Amenhotep III's tomb is amazingly undecorated and unfinished, and his body in extremely unusual poor condition.

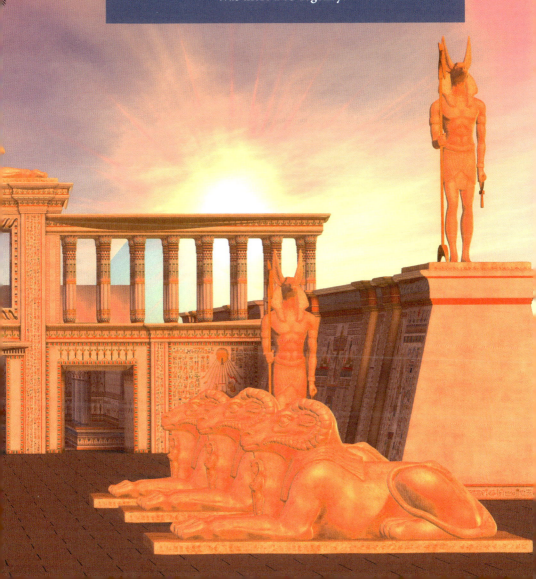

Chapter 4

THE SHAMED EXODUS PHAROAH

Amenhotep's exceedingly high status

How he was shamed after the Exodus

Amenhotep's unique mummy

Amenhotep's unusual tomb

The demise of the firstborn Crown Prince

Was there a co-regency?

AMENHOTEP III'S SUPREME STATUS

AMENHOTEP III 'the magnificent' had been officially considered to be a living manifestation of the creator god Ra (Re), particularly in his manifestation as the sun's disk, Aten, and hence was a living embodiment of all the gods of Egypt, their 'living image' on earth... there were multiple images of almost all the gods in the likeness of this great king, also hundreds of lioness-headed black Sekhmet statues holding the *ankh* and featuring the sun; and several kilometres of sculptures of the king in animal form, such as andro-sphinxes, criosphinxes, rams, jackals, lions and even falcons, vultures, and serpents, which guarded the avenues leading to his temple complexes. The inscriptions, style, and iconography indicate that most of this sculpture was prepared before the king's 30th year, in preparation for his jubilee that year. Amenhotep III also took on the role of Ptah, creator of the gods as defined in the Memphite Theology, gathering the images of all the gods and uniting with them himself as part of his jubilee celebration and deification.

A fine statue of Amenhotep III currently displayed in the Baltimore Museum.

Several sculptures celebrating a deified Amenhotep III, datable by their unusual style, were produced also after that first jubilee. For example, a remarkable quartzite statue of the king from the Luxor temple and now on display in the 'Cachette' gallery of Luxor Museum, depicts him in the 'rejuvenation' or 'deification' style of his last decade. With the powerful body of a younger man and ultra-large eyes that cunningly heighten the effect of his supposed youthfulness, Amenhotep III wears a kilt with uraei and falcon feathers. The statue is essentially a representation of the king as the solar deity, and is named: *"Ruler of the Nine Bows, Dazzling Aten of all lands, whose Uraeus illuminates the Two Banks".* It was set up in his Luxor temple and was no doubt the centre-piece of Amenhotep III's cult there, just as other statues of the deified king in many different forms and scales were set up at this time in all the major religious centres, most of them in sparkling quartzite, a stone fittingly associated with a sun god.

British Museum EA 2275 in black steatite, depicts Amenhotep III in a long pleated kilt with an elaborate sporran holding a heqa-sceptre. The wide belts, sporran and looped sashes, the cords with papyrus umbels, are all representative of the 'deification' style of the king's later years.

Amenhotep was noted especially for his unprecedented building schemes, whereas his predecessor Amenhotep II had been noted for his military conquests. This too fits with the *Bible's* accounts of this great 'Exodus' Pharoah.

His people may well also have noted that Amenhotep III rarely went on any international diplomatic missions; he evidently only went to Sidon once, and maybe took no other trip into Canaan during his long kingship. The Amarna letters indicate a very high level of respect for him and his massive army, as well as for his abundant and generous gifts of gold, of course!

HOW HE WAS VIEWED AFTER THE EXODUS

What an emotional conflict Akhenaten must have had, regarding his late father; on the one hand, viewing him as blasphemous in his highly active support and embodiment of the 'false' gods, yet recognising his major achievements and representation of Aten, albeit in an earlier composite form.

Publicly for a while at least, there was likely to have been underlying resentment of, and disappointment at, Amenhotep III's kingship with its evident loss of the entire army, and national pride, so it is understandable that we do find Akhenaten's attempts to restore a rather better posthumous view of his father especially as a 'god' in later Amarna years.

Many statues of Pharoah Amenhotep III were later re-modelled to depict Rameses II.

Amenhotep III's posterity does seem to have been in some disgrace, as many later kings used Amenhotep III's huge funerary temple as a ready source of 'instant' statuary.

Rameses II removed six Amenhotep III granite statues while adding to his famed Luxor temple, and even had his predecessor's distinctive facial features replaced with his own, including notably his thinner lips ... at least one of the seated colossi in his 'Ramesseum' funerary temple had been re-carved in this way. Even the famous fallen granite colossus is thought to be actually Amenhotep III, not Rameses. Also, Merneptah, a son of Rameses II, adapted many Amenhotep III statues with his own cartouche. Massive limestone figures of Amenhotep III with his associated gods were moved to Merneptah's funerary temple, which was itself largely made up of blocks re-used from Amenhotep III buildings. What disgust they seem to have had for his memory!

The following pages indicate other ways that show a surprisingly inglorious perception of the people's late king, at the time. His mummy was especially badly treated, and his tomb.

AMENHOTEP III'S MUMMY

The words *mom* or *mummia* are Arabic words with five different meanings usually describing a pissasphalt or natural pitch (*mummia*) that is excreted from rocks in the middle east, but also referring to honeybee wax (*mom*) used as a preservative, bitumen (red *mummia*, or *qifr)* used profusely in later times in mummification, aromatic resin (*qitran*) from cedars or conifers, and sea resin or asphalt (*zift*).

Amenhotep III mummy has the bones and a toe of another human inside it, and pebbles wrapped in bandages, as well as evidence of a highly unusual wet-natron treatment.

Joann Fletcher says that Alfred Lucas, a chemist and Director of the Chemical Department of the Egyptian government at the time of Howard Carter, with whom he worked in 1922, noticed a unique 'snowflake' pattern on the skin of the arms of Amenhotep III's mummy. It seems that this mummy was treated quite differently to much later 19th Dynasty resin-filled mummies. The effervescence causing the snowflake effect must have been caused by the presence of much more water, such as using natron salt in a solution, in a bath—a unique use of liquid natron.

It is likely that his skin would have been first rubbed with vegetable oil and resin, then the body immersed in a strong natron bath before being stuffed with much more resin than was commonly used at that time.

There is total consensus on the understanding that Amenhotep's mummy was processed in a unique manner. Recent re-evaluation of 18th Dynasty mummies by the *American Association of Physical Anthropologists,* using new scientific disciplines and methods such as DNA-profiling, CT-scanning was published in their Journal[1].

Amenhotep III mummy is strangely mutilated, embalmed in a way that was unprecedented, and shows evidence of great neglect and disrespect.

> *"The wrappings were opened by Grafton Smith in September 23, 1905 and revealed a body in a bad condition, somewhere between fully preserved mummy and skeleton[2]. Smith assumed that the body was exposed and severely damaged by ancient grave robbers. The head was broken off, and most of the soft tissue from the face is gone. The right leg was also broken away from the trunk, and part of the foot is missing. The embalmers tied the fragments of the body together with bandages. Inside the body cavity, there were bones from birds, a human big toe, and parts of an arm (ulna and radius). The embalmers basically had 'taped' the mummy together and tried to restore a lifelike appearance by placing a resinous mass of subcutaneous stuffing in the legs, arms, and neck".*

The mummy was found in KV35 but is now in the Cairo Museum. It is worth reading the full detailed unwrapping report by Grafton Smith from 1905, which still has the only set of direct photographs published on its pages[2]. It is readily available. The scientists conclude that a *'re-evaluation of the Amarna age'* needed!! Here are some of the puzzling features:

> *"Genetic studies have indicated that mummy CG 61074 comes from the 18th Dynasty, and this raises several issues: why did the embalmers develop this new technique of stuffing to achieve a life-like appearance and why was this new style then abandoned until it reappeared three centuries later as state-of-the-art mummification of the 21st Dynasty? It is highly unlikely that the subcutaneous stuffing with resinous material was carried out on dry mummified tissue some 300 years later during restoration, which would severely damage the friable dry tissue. The stuffing of CG 61074 is most likely to have been carried out during the original mummification process in an attempt to create a lifelike appearance."*

The embalmers had unusually packed the skin of the deceased king with a new resinous material, and the body seems 'bloated'. His body also had a broken rib and bones, leg and head[3] severed from the body, and almost the whole front of his body missing; bits of pebble had been wrapped into his body, and bird legs, and a stray big toe from another human; he appears to have died at the age of around 40-50 with no clear cause of death.

The report says,

> *"Then another bandage wound around the legs spirally down to the feet and then back again beyond the knees, there were pieces of pebble in this bandage... The broken fragments of the body were held together by means of three bandages tied around them. Among the lumps of resin-impregnated linen inside the body cavity were found the leg bone of a fowl and another bird's limb bone, a human great toe, and a left ulnar and radius."*

The mummy had been placed in a wooden coffin originally intended for the reburial of Seti II, and the container of the coffin bore the name of Rameses III. Another strange situation, using a secondhand coffin.

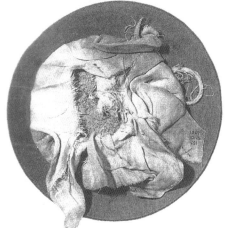

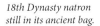

18th Dynasty natron still in its ancient bag.

AMENHOTEP III'S TOMB

Opposite page:

Photo of Amenhotep III mummy taken much more recently.

Below:

Diagram of KV22, the original tomb of Amenhotep III showing almost every space as undecorated.

Amenhotep III was originally buried in WV22 (West Valley) at a remote end, then transferred later to the main Valley (KV35) in the 21st Dynasty.

Halfway through his original tomb, it is quite remarkable that the space is undecorated; the tomb is startlingly unimaginative, especially given the high historical status of this 'magnificent' and 'greatest' Pharoah. Experts have been disappointed by the great poverty and unimaginative character of his original tomb, while the carving out of the shafts and rooms is nonetheless well done and such decoration as there is, exhibits very high quality, probably being worked upon during his lifetime. Strangely, a high quality chariot hub was also found in the tomb.

None of the painted scenes has been engraved, strangely. You get the impression that most of the work was done in haste and a limited time, with little incentive to give it the usual attention and respect, especially considering the opulent magnificence of his reign, and that much of the intended decoration has never been completed. Several rooms have only three of their four walls with any decoration[4]. Some main areas have none.

On the diagram below, the many spaces that are undecorated (shown in bolder type, with asterisked spaces having only three of their four walls decorated) include A, B, C, D, E*, Ea, F, G, H, I*, Ja, Jb, Jbb, Jc, Jcc, Jd and Je.

The décor of the tomb is quite bland, even bare; there is just a brief inscription in black on a white painted background!

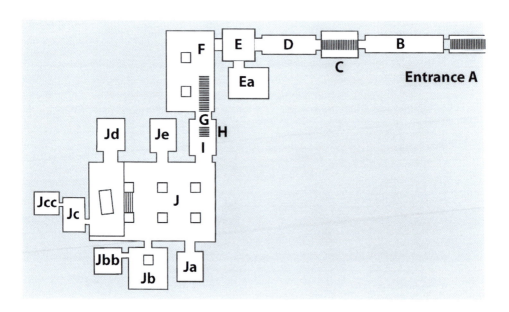

Experts[5] say that it is *"apparent that these mummies, including Amenhotep III, had been hidden by priests of 21st Dynasty."*

Amenhotep's original coffin had disappeared. The granite lid is in 50 pieces, and his mummy found in the tomb of Amenhotep II in a box made for Rameses III with a lid made over for Seti II and then docketed for Amenhotep III.

His final coffin is quite crude; probably a re-used one of Rameses III, damaged before its use, with Amenhotep's body re-buried.

The name of his father Thutmosis IV was found[6] in the foundation deposits, thus it would appear the tomb was started by him. The entrance is quite unimposing, given that this great Pharaoh was famous especially for the scale and grandeur of his building works. The entry stairways and corridors are quite without decoration.

Just imagine the people's hatred of this previously deified king; how tricked they must have felt; how tragically sad many must have been having lost their mighty military relatives; how confused they must have been, not understanding this new Aten 'religion' any more than they really ever had a grasp of the old one... and how many of them will have lost their employment after the purge of disgraced temples, priests and support systems.

Their *corps d'elite* had gone, many with royal connections with fancy new-tech chariots, leaders in the army, with men like Yuya and Ay as examples of this class, whilst just a few would likely have remained back at base in administrative roles.

Why is the great Amenhotep III's tomb so unfinished and undecorated?

Even the king's *maryann* elite archer-charioteers must have been wiped out; these were the *Star Wars* fighters of the era; superfast arrows being shot from flying six-spoked 'panzer' chariots, with weapons re-loading several times a minute.

Recent photo, with temporary recent supports also shown.

His burial contrasts starkly with that of Yuya and Thuya, parents of Queen Tiye. Though they were commoners, this indeed being rare in the Valley of the Kings, they are both found in the finest coffins, and now viewable in Cairo Museum.

However, Amenhotep III's long-prepared funerary temple at Western Thebes was architecturally lavish, gold-lined, the best ever, as you would expect; yet only two colossi remain now... what a poor way to treat what must have been Egypt's greatest ever Pharoah!

THE DEATH OF THE FIRSTBORN SON

One of the most amazing facts is the relatively well-documented existence of Crown Prince Djhutmose[8] ('B')[7], the firstborn son of Amenhotep III; if the Hebrew *Bible* is correct, he would have died quite young and his second-born brother would likely have taken the throne; this is exactly what happened!

The Crown Prince's mummy is thought to be the one re-buried appropriately alongside his mother, Queen Tiye, and close to his father, Amenhotep III. He was initially buried at Waset and re-buried later alongside his mother. See photos on pages 5 and 23 of this book.

He must have had special prominence as a boy, mostly at the capital Memphis; with very high titles, *"The Crown Prince, Overseer of the Priests of Upper and Lower Egypt, High Priest of Ptah, and sem-priest of Ptah,"* — even at this young age, one of the most powerful males in the world, head of a prominent cult and with prime responsibility for every priest in the land!   He would have been King Djhutmosis V if he had lived long enough to become king.

In contrast, Akhenaten does not feature anywhere as a boy, with only brief mention on a jar inscription (now displayed in the Louvre N 394 1A-D) *"the estate of the king's son, Amenhotep".* The focus must always have been on the Crown Prince Djhutmose, the firstborn, who would have been groomed for his intended later more prominent royal role; he seems already to have been part of his father's more assertive grand plan.

He is even credited with the radical new design of a mausoleum for the Apis bulls, a design which continued to be used until the late Ptolemaic era. For a description of this, and illustration, go to Aidan Dodsons book[6]. This new design accompanied a new tradition for the internment of sacred Apis bulls, using his magnificently designed and constructed mausoleum built at Mit Rahina, Saqqara. It comprised an elevated stone platform approached by a flight of steps, on top of which stood a classic stone chapel with fluted columns and relief-clad walls. The Prince is shown on these reliefs, with his father, offering incense to his sacred bull. A similar relief fragment stands in the Munich museum. The burial site itself is beneath the chapel, at the foot of a sloping passageway, in a rectangular chamber containing stone and pottery vessels some of which are inscribed with the Prince's name; also four canopic jars relate to him, now stored in the Louvre.

Crown Prince Djhutmose is now well documented as the firstborn son of Amenhotep III, and who died of no known cause as a young teenager.

Evidence for the Prince's identity comes from four main artefacts; he was laid to rest at Memphis near his pet cat *'Ta-Miu'* which has a tiny limestone sarcophagus, which bears the Prince's official titles *"The Crown Prince, Overseer of the Priests of Upper and Lower Egypt, High Priest of Ptah, and sem priest of Ptah,"* together with the cat's name almost a dozen times. This sarcophagus now resides in the Cairo Museum [CG 5003 = JE 30172].

The cat is portrayed in mummified form alongside Osiris and Nephthys in typical contemporary style, with prayers indicated as being offered to the sky goddess Nut.

The sarcophagus of lost firstborn son and royal heir Crown Prince Djhutmose's beloved cat Ta-Miu, probably prepared in the Prince's lifetime

So, even the cat is involved in a (later) disgraced religion; the cat also being associated with the sun-god Re, as shown on the *Book of the Dead*. Other gods used cats as their symbol, including the fearsome Sekhmet lioness holding the ankh, and the goddess Bastet.

The cat sarcophagus conclusively proves that this Prince was the eldest son of Amenhotep III, as it gives his title as 'Crown Prince'.

Also portraying the Prince is the 'corn-grinding statuette' now in the Louvre [N 792=E 2749] along with 7 associated pairs of calcite or pottery vases.

If the Crown Prince was between age 11 and 20 when he died, Akhenaten (named 'Amen-Hotep' at the time), must have been between the ages of 10 and 19 upon taking over the kingship, at least ruling in name whilst his mother dealt with any important dialogue (as reflected in the Amarna letters). They were perhaps more likely to have been towards the upper end of this age range though, as suggested by the Crown Prince's mature work in designing and revising the Apis temple and procedure.

The Prince then disappears suddenly and mysteriously from all records, and his younger brother Akhenaten takes his royal place.

Females cannot have been counted as 'firstborn'; the plagues evidently killed Pharoah's firstborn son, but not the daughters.

'Corn-grinding statuette' of the first-born Crown Prince Djhutmose, now in the Louvre museum.

These statuettes were placed inside tombs as servants for the supposed afterlife.

Far right: Crown Prince Djhutmose was evidently an avid cat-lover; this is Bastet, a cat-inspired god of Egypt

WAS THERE A CO-REGENCY OF AMENHOTEP III AND IV?

Debates about a co-regency of Amenhoteps III and IV still rage, despite a confident but questioned proclamation by Mohamed Ibrahim Ali, head of the Egyptian Antiquities Ministry, in 2014[10] that 'conclusive' evidence for a co-regency had been found in a 1978 dig. The doubt exists though because the 'Amen-Hotep-Huy' tomb they dated to the 30th year of Amenhotep III still apparently has no evidence for that dating, and its occupant may have been alive well beyond year 35; he was supervising the Gebel El Silsila quarry works through much of both reigns. The fact that the tomb features cartouches of both Amenhotep III and IV simply shows surely that Huy worked under both kings, not necessarily at the same time. They are both depicted as kings, quite naturally, in hindsight. Before this find, the hints at a co-regency were very slender.

Amenhotep III and Queen Tiye.

(Berlin Museum)

The argument for

In addition to the aforementioned Huy cartouches, there are some ambiguous hints at a possible co-regency.

At Amarna, there is a lintel scene preserved in the tomb of Huya, the Steward of Queen Tiye, which is dated after Akhenaten's year 9 (according to the late form of the Aten's name). Amenhotep III is represented as 'living' and shown rather larger than Akhenaten, as also is his throne. The lintel is in two halves, depicting the two royal families back-to-back: one side shows Akhenaten, Nefertiti, and their four royal daughters, and on the other is Amenhotep III, with Queen Tiye and a young daughter. The right hands of both Tiye and her daughter are raised up in worship and have been interpreted as indications both that Amenhotep III is dead, or alternatively that his memory is being glorified long after death.

Similarly, a carved sandstone stele [BM 57399] excavated by the *Egypt Exploration Society* in the House of Panehsy, High Priest of the Aten at Amarna has been interpreted both as evidence that Amenhotep III was still alive, and also the opposite view, that the stela is homage to the deceased king, intended to be part of a 'cult of the dead king', improving his posterity, and using his throne name 'Neb-Maat-Ra' rather than Amen, and the featured Aten name is a later form (9th yr onwards).

Another line of support is the matching of the 3-yearly sed feasts between the two kings, being the 30th, 34th and 37th regnal years of Amenhotep seeming to match the years 5, 9 and 12 of Akhenaten; but the simple maths here is that Akhenaten was mimicking the previously traditional 3-yearly cycle, so they were bound to line up, if indeed Akhenaten did actually have 3 sed-feasts, as there is only scant ambiguous evidence that this was the case.

The argument against

Against it is the more recently published photo of an original date on Amarna letter EA26 (see picture here) as 'Year 2' in Egyptian script, showing that its message of a recent and tragic death of the previous Pharoah must still have been fresh in minds within two years of Akhenaten's accession.

That letter from Tushratta shows, by using his new throne name, that Akhenaten is nominally ruling at the time of condolence for the loss of Amenhotep III, with widow Tiye being in charge with some authority or influence over the young son, known as Amenhotep IV.

Amarna letter EA29, now written to Akhenaten about death of the king (obviously the previous king) being tragic when he 'went to' his ('fate') death;

'Year 2' inscription on the edge of Amarna letter EA26, showing how the tragic death of the previous Pharoah was probably still fresh in the minds of all, within two years of the accession of Akhenaten.

"When my brother, [Amenhotep III], went to his fate it was reported. When I heard what was reported... I grieved, saying, "Let even me be dead, or let 10,000 be dead in my country, and in my brother's country 10,000 as well, but let my brother, whom I love and who loves me, be alive as long as heaven and earth."

We have a letter, therefore, that gives us some context about the death of Amenhotep III which, if he indeed was the Pharaoh of the Exodus could be consistent with his death in the Red Sea, or at least not contradictory. He thus literally 'went to' his tragic death or 'fate'.

Amenhotep III's wife Tiye evidently took over rulership for a while at end of his reign, and received at least one of the Amarna letters (EA26) on a king's behalf; as you'd expect, if the king died suddenly, and his first son was killed, exactly as outlined in the book of Exodus; a young second-born son would take some time to prepare or be old enough to take responsibility as the new king. This was Akhenaten, quite unprepared for royal leadership.

Also against are the many colossi of Akhenaten from the early constructions at Karnak East, depicting him alone holding the ruler's authoritative crook and flail without reference to any co-regent.

Also, there would be a contradiction in the status of Amenhotep, as he says he IS the god at Waset, yet Akhenaten declared the sun-disk to be an abstract figure in those later years, with the king merely as his son. If they shared a sed-feast, it would have been more confusing than ever, and not at all likely.

Crown Prince Djhutmose must have been groomed as 'king designate' years before Akhenaten reigned, thus he would be more likely to have been a co-regent than Akhenaten.

Only Akhenaten's name, rather than both, is removed from most inscriptions in the later restitution years.

There is no correspondence between the two.

No other inscription is known to have the two together.

Also, the circumstantial evidence in this book far outweighs the idea that the Exodus king Amenhotep III continued living and reigned with Akhenaten.

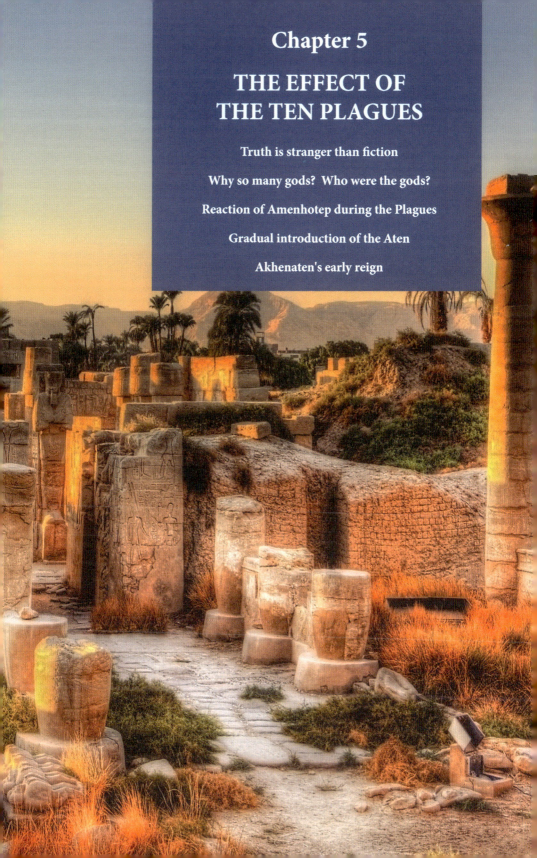

Chapter 5

THE EFFECT OF
THE TEN PLAGUES

Truth is stranger than fiction

Why so many gods? Who were the gods?

Reaction of Amenhotep during the Plagues

Gradual introduction of the Aten

Akhenaten's early reign

I T THUS SEEMS extremely likely that the Ten Plagues, or something equally devastating, were the primary reason for Akhenaten's destruction of the gods, ruined in credibility as they were now. Why else, after all the centuries of devotion and offerings, with a populace seeming to be in high spirits in an Egypt at its peak, and with a king more successful than any previous, and religion so prosperous, could Akhenaten have reason to eliminate them?

If it were just a matter of claiming Amun's foreign income for the government rather than enriching the priests, then surely a royal proclamation—a new law—could quite easily have been promulgated.

If the many pagan priests were getting too militant or powerful, he need not have moved elsewhere and en-acted such a sudden and complete revolution. As king, he could hire and fire, as he frequently did. During the reign of Amenhotep III, moves had already been made to restrict the power of the priests, and the king and his family had ultimate influence and authority over the personnel there already.

Immediately following the tenth Plague, the Hebrews are said to have left Egypt, with the strong blessing of most of the Egyptians, many of whom gave them clothing and valuables, and in fact, a huge number of them went with the fleeing Hebrews, becoming a *'mixed company'*[1] of about three million. One item of evidence for this has been dem-onstrated by Rosalie David[2], in her excavations at Kahun, near Waset, where there was, she says, a sudden leaving of Semitic people from that site. According to her 1986 book *Pyramid Builders of Ancient Egypt, page 199*:

Amun, the most reviled god of Egypt under the new regime.

Amun had been the chief of all the gods, merging his identity with many others at various times, especially as Amun-Ra.

"*the quantity, range and type of articles of everyday use which were left behind in the houses may indeed suggest that the departure [of the workmen] was sudden and unpremeditated*".

'GODS'... WHAT ARE THEY?

Basically, a god is something that is worshipped, or as Donald Redford lu-cidly defines it, a 'target of devotion'[3]. This suggests that the religious aspect or 'godship' is at least perceived in the mind of a worshipper, rather than in the god's mind if any! But where we are referring to something already acknowledged as being worshipped by many, the material culture relating to that god becomes a focus of interest, as to whether the god has any real supernatural power or legitimate hold over its worshippers, in fact.

Here, then, is a need to outline what the *Bible* says about 'gods'... where else would you look for an authoritative insight on such a topic?

Egyptian history seems to have started around 2300 BCE. Before that, we are in the realms of 'pre-history', as it is called.

People in Egypt thought their gods had real power; they approached them to determine justice or remedy... fifteen ancient letters have been found[4], written to dead relatives dating back almost to the pre-historic Old Kingdom asking the SPIRITS to help them with their current issues! Some 'letters' were written on bowls, also linen and papyrus; most were left at a tomb on celebration days, with food. This indicates a long-held belief that there really were living 'gods' (demons) that at one time had interacted with humans.[5]

Quite amazingly, the *Bible* in Genesis chapter six gives an insight as to the probable origin of these gods, or at least the concept of their old 'gods' with characteristics of animals as well as humans, and with supernatural powers. Genesis 6 starts (paraphrased):

> *"When men started to increase on the surface of the ground, and daughters were born to them, some sons of God saw how beautiful the daughters of men were and took wives for themselves, all whom they chose ... It was then, and after that too, that the Nephilim appeared on earth—when the divine beings had relations with the daughters of men, and bore them sons. They were the mighty ones of old, the men of fame."*

These beings had apparently actually lived both in 'heaven' and earth, and when they 'died' they were said to have gone back to 'heaven' and lived on in another form. This matches the myth of Ra also. This was very likely also the basis of the many later Greek myths, with their larger than life characters and exploits; Hercules, Atlas, Cronos, Orpheus, Dionysius, and many more.

Stele of woman kneeling before two ancestor busts; in British Museum.

'Demi-gods' and 'gods' were described as powerful rulers, by Manetho, the *Bible*, the *Turin King List*, Greek and Egyptian mythologies. Amazing, is it not, that these two unlikely classifications are consistently featured in unrelated accounts?

The *Turin King List* (dated to Rameses II reign) begins with a list of ancient 'gods' as though they were Pharoahs at the start of what is termed the 'Old Kingdom', or 'pre-Dynastic' from around 3500 - 2300 BCE.

The presence, in Akhenaten's tomb, of 1000-year-old stone bowls with names from the ancient 4th Dynasty could indicate there was an awareness of frightful spirit 'sons of God' who became powerful gods before the global flood in the early 3rd millennium BCE, described in Genesis 6, and which laid the basis for the entire Greek mythology relating to 'gods' who had miraculous powers of materialization as well as 'demi-gods' having superhuman

strength. These ancient 'gods' are referred to as the 'imperishable ones' by the Egyptians, in recognition of the belief that the ancient supernatural pre-flood gods had become stars in heaven rather than experiencing real death, and they often aligned their pyramids with these constellations because of this. These stars were thought of as 'watchers'[6] as they never dipped below the horizon, as though they were actually the ancient 'gods'.

In Hesiod's *'Theogony',* and other Greek writings, these ones were often called 'deathless ones' and 'watchers' because of their ability to de-materialise back into the spirit realm.

Thoth, the baboon, supposedly maintained the universe and created writing.

WHY SO MANY GODS?

There were at least 500 gods in most periods of ancient Egypt; some say up to 2000, if you count demons, demi-gods and combination gods, trinities and godheads, constantly changing, morphing into each other, changing names and often having alternative names in other city-states both in Egypt and often elsewhere. Babylon and Sumer had very similar gods from the start, as did to a lesser extent the peoples in Canaan. It must have been extremely confusing for everyone, although it appears that each family focused on just one, or a very few, favourite gods to care for them in much the same way as Roman Catholics today often have a favourite 'saint' they pray to, focussing on a particular aspect of life or admired quality.

The meaning of the word 'heiroglyphs' (Greek) is 'words of the gods', *medu netjer* in Egyptian; a form of sacred writing only understood by the elite—the 'gods'—at an early time in Egypt's [pre-]history! The understanding of this style of writing was long hidden from anyone's knowledge until young Champollion, that young whizz-kid of language, deciphered most of it in and around the year 1822 CE.

Early in Egyptian history, various versions of god configurations arose, different in Memphis, Esna, Hermopolis and (later) Edfu; similar also in Babylon and other areas, where each city-state would have its own version of the gods, often trinities, apparently in memory of the pre-Flood 'gods', who appear to have been in three groups, under three 'senior' demons - a pattern found in several ancient superstitions.

Many of the formats were reflected in Babylon too, usually with different names. From Babylon (Babel[7]) these ideas spread around the young expanding world, accelerated by the new diversity of language, as Genesis 10 says:

> *"These were the families, according to their tongues, and according to their nations, and from these the nations branched out in the earth after the Flood."*

Heliopolis (the biblical 'On') seems to be one of the very earliest centres of this worship, with 'Atum' having a mythological 'seed' as the first ever couple, Tefnut & Shu; they had mythological offspring Geb & Nut; they, in turn, had Osiris, Isis, Seth, and Nephthys. There was no place for an atheist here!

"Cosmogonic thought is basic to Egyptian religion," says Yves Bonnefoy in his major work *Mythologies*[8]. Astronomy was very sophisticated back then, with amazing insight into the positions and movements of the stars, clearly visible only after the global flood of the early 3rd millennium had brought down the massive ancient water-vapour canopy described in Gen 1:7.   Planispheres seem to date only from around this time, with their recording of star and constellation movements across the observed sky. Alexander the Great collected hundreds of these, the oldest apparently going back to around 2200 BCE.

Even the Hebrews often had 'other' gods; large numbers of teraphim have been found throughout ancient Israel villages, as they too attempted to obtain the favour of various local baals.

WHO WERE EGYPT'S GODS?

Most significantly, there were thought to be four phases of the major Sun god, just prior to Akhenaten's time:

> Horakhty represented the rising sun, above the 'horizon'.
> Ra, the main course of the sun across the sky.
> Aten was the highest point of the sun in the sky.
> Atum, the fading sun, completion of 'all' the cycle.

Wadjet, supposed protector of Egypt and childbirth. Also known as the 'eye of Ra'

The first two made up 'Amun' at a later time, and at the time of Amenhotep, the High Priest of Amun was said to be the 'overseer of the priests of all the gods'. Amun ('great god') was particularly 'dark' and 'hidden' and became the main target of Akhenaten's wrath.

These also were, as a combination, some of the nine gods that made up the Ennead of Heliopolis, the others being Shu, Tefnut, Geb, Nut, Osiris, Isis, and Set.

Aten [properly associated with 'Ra-Horakhty' at the time of Amenhotep III] was seen by Akhenaten to be uniquely universal; that is, not just for Egypt; the idea seems to have developed gradually that '*the Aten*' (the sun disc) was a combination of the Big Four, for acceptance by Upper Egypt (where they predominantly worshipped

Ra (Re) as the main god, with Horus, Amun, Osiris, or Ra as Amun-Ra; — they couldn't spell!) and Lower Egypt (where they mostly worshipped Ra-Horakhty–Horus, or Ra-Horus-Aten as the main gods at the time) and was falcon-headed until the Gem-pa-Aten festival of Akhenaten's early reign, where suddenly '*the* Aten' was presented as an acceptable embodiment of all of these, being the highest representation of all the sun gods, and making them redundant.

Aten was not historically linked to any particular city or area, unlike all other gods; maybe this made his identity more acceptable to all Egyptians when Akhenaten featured the nameless Aten disc as a re-placement for all the other regional gods, presenting 'him' as a god from another level, able to impact on human life.

Thus Aten was now presented in a completely new way, ditch-ing the falcon-headed man and physical idolatry; no need for his priests to wash and prepare 'him' every morning; this was a god that could supposedly look after 'himself' as well as everyone else! Except for the fact that 'he' couldn't.

These gods couldn't even cancel themselves, or merge them-selves with others; it was all in the minds of the people!

Ptah, the creator god, and one of Egypt's primary gods.

Since the 12th Dynasty, 500 years earlier, Aten had been simply a facet of Ra, and acceptable as male or female, or preferably both together! His previous depiction as a falcon-headed man was the same as Horus and Horakhty ('Ra-Horakhty' means 'Ra is Horus of the Horizon'). Confused? You should be! No doubt the Egyptian people were too.

Fact is, the Aten was just as useless as all the others, as useless as it always had been previously, despite the new spin. What was new was a sudden need and urgent attempt to recognise and make sense of the Hebrew victory, after the Ten Plagues and the Exodus. You could say that Akhenaten was a 'Great Pretender'... combining some of the gods but with no real substance; the Aten wasn't the actual power of YHWH that they had witnessed in the escape of the Hebrews. Akhenaten made only a feeble attempt at liturgy or explana-tion of heritage or mythology relating to the newly styled Aten, unlike that provided by Israel's God for his people. No holy book, nor writings, that we know of, other than scant ideas in the two Aten 'Hymns' and the 'early proc-lamation' inscribed on three boundary stelae written on arrival at Amarna.

It would be true to say that in the later years of Amenhotep III there was a gradual move towards a combination of gods, a recognition perhaps that maybe there was just one big One, as perhaps those influential monotheists Moses and Joseph must have been at least hinting at from earliest times! Maybe, therefore, it had to do with these influences from Hebrew-Israelite personnel very close to the royals for the past four generations; not only Jo-seph and Moses but Levi and Aaron not to mention old Abraham, that visiting expert astronomer from Ur, expert in mathematics, astronomy and monothe-ism. Josephus tells much more about that immensely clever, respected and influential character[9].

Amenhotep III thought of himself as god in his own lifetime, and especially from his 30th year and his public deification. Some gods were combined into him as part of 'Aten', especially the Ptah-Sokar-Osiris combo. They loved their trinities! They also had Amen, Mut and (son) Khonsu; Osiris, Horus and Isis; (Atum) Shu, Tefnut and Mahet; Amun, Ra and Ptah; Isis, Horus and Serapis (probably the basis of the 'IHS' idea, from this later Greek adaptation of the earlier main Egyptian trinity with Osiris)[10].

Waset (later known as Thebes) became the real centre of these god combinations, and thousands of priests and support staff must have been employed in all these temples and shrines; many of the minor gods also came to have small chapels within the precincts of Amun's temples at Waset. It could be that after the revolution of Akhenaten, many of these priests found re-employment in his huge new temples, where as many as 3,000 offerings tables needed servicing in one temple alone, for a kind of religious 'fast food' service!

Akhenaten did have a scant scripture text that partially defined his teleological doctrine of the-Aten as a personal reflection of the world through his eyes, which is reflected within two important works – the Boundary Stela-'M' at Amarna (unfortunately this stela, which had deeper insights into his motivation, deteriorated badly in antiquity[11]) and most importantly the *Great-Hymn-to-the-Aten* inscribed within Ay's tomb[12] - there are many similar stelae and hymns which echo these texts; Ay's tomb is dated between the 5th and 9th regnal years of Akhenaten.

Ptah-Sokar-Osiris statue currently at National Museums Scotland

Assmann[13] described Aten theology as being firstly an embryonic treatise (as an evolution of Heliopolitan creation-myths) and secondly a statement of the world's harmony – he paraphrases it as *"natural philosophy"*... when people get sick of their ineffective and remote 'gods' they turn in preference to nature worship, which is less tricky and much more peaceful.

The continual re-development of the gods of Egypt is outside the scope or need of this book. See G Mumford's thesis on that topic and notes on his lectures [14].

Egyptians, much like most other peoples, felt a constant need to respect the 'gods', in order to reap perceived benefits in agriculture, rainfall, weather, personal relationships and fortune, as well as an eye on the perceived heavenly 'after-life'.

Even the more well-informed Hebrews frequently reverted to worship of the local Semitic Baals in Canaan, mostly for reasons of agriculture, and lack of faith in their own God.

Top:
Baal 'storm god' from Canaan; sometimes worshipped by ancient Israelites.

Right:
Akhenaten and Nefertiti make offerings to their divine counterparts Shu and Tefnut

Below:
Amarna as it is today

THE TEN PLAGUES

The key point here is that all of the gods of Egypt were unable to stop these 10 Plagues; time after time   they proved they had no power over any aspects of life, compared with the God of the Hebrews who was able to start and stop each Plague.

1. NILE BLOOD; Ex 7:19-24 This would have greatly discredited Hapi [god of Nile]; Amun [king of all gods]; Anuket [goddess of Nile]; Sobek [god of crocodiles]; Tefnut [goddess of water]; Hu [god of the spoken word].

2. FROGS; Ex 8:1-6 This would have greatly discredited Osiris [creator god], Ptah[supreme god]; Heket [goddess of frogs].

3. GNATS; Ex 8:12-13 This would have greatly discredited Thoth [god of magic]; Geb [god of earth]; Shu [god of the air]; Baal [storm and sky god];

4. GADFLIES Ex 8:19-20 This would have greatly discredited Horus [god of lower Egypt]; Baal [storm and sky god].

5. LIVESTOCK; Ex 9:6 This would have greatly discredited Hathor [cow god]; Nut [cow in sky]; Shed [god to save people from misfortune].

6. BOILS; Ex 9:10,11 This would have greatly discredited Amun-Ra [main god]; Isis [goddess of healing]; Serket [goddess for protection]; Sekhmet [goddess for healing and life].

7. HAIL; Ex 9:25 This would have greatly discredited Shu [god of the air]; Reshpu [god of conflict]; Tefnut [god of weather].

8. LOCUSTS; Ex 10:12-15 This would have greatly discredited Min [god of harvest]; Osiris [god of vegetation]; Horus [god of the sky]; Shu [god of the air]; Min [god of crops].

9. DARKNESS; Ex 10:21-2   This would have greatly discredited Ra (main sun god); Sekhmet [a solar goddess]; Thoth [moon god]; Khepri [a sun god]; Khnum [sun god of the evening]; Khonsu [moon god]; Nut [goddess of the sky]; Seth [god of change, storms].

10. FIRSTBORN MALES KILLED Ex 12:29,30 This would have greatly discredited Ra [god's offspring]; Bes [god of the royals]; Buto [king protector]; Osiris [god of the dead & resurrection]; Bastet [protector of children]; Wadjet [goddess of protection]; Werethek-au [god to protect king]; Wepawet [god of domestic protection]; Wenut [god of protection]; Waset [god of protecting the young]; Sed [a god of the firstborn]; Sokar [god of resurrection];

Crown Prince Djhutmose, the firstborn son of Amenhotep III who died mysteriously at a young age.

His mummy lies next to his mother, and in close proximity to his father Amenhotep III.

Amenhotep III's Malkata Palace shown in this modern painting; he made lavish use of gold, silver and precious stones during his reign.

REACTION OF AMENHOTEP III TO THE TEN PLAGUES

Amenhotep III had deified himself in his final years; the first one ever to do so! Asserting himself to be so much stronger, he claimed to be a 'joint god with Amun' at the time of his first sed-feast, in his 30th year as king; he took on a new throne name Neb-maat-Ra.

We may ask ourselves, why did he feel the need to do this? Was there a new threat of supreme godship, of sovereignty, or a tussle with the fabulously wealthy and powerful priests?

Strange also that Amenhotep held three sed-feasts in quick succession; in his 30th, 34th, and 37th years. Other Pharoahs had not done this *'since the time of the ancestors'*, and needed to be enacted *'in accordance with writings of old'*. His 'Mansion of Rejoicing' was specially commissioned, but his queen Tiye seems not to have been happy with it.

He must have been all too aware, and probably fearful, of the name of the Hebrew's mighty God; it was evidently spoken frequently in his court.

Exodus examples where YHWH's name is specifically spoken in Pharoah's presence, either by him, his servants, soldiers or by Moses:

Exodus 10:3,7,8,10,11,16,24,25,26

(Moses) *"Thus says YHWH, the God of the Hebrews, 'How long will you refuse.."*

(Pharoah's courtiers) *"How long shall this one be a snare to us? Let the men go to serve YHWH their God!"*

(Pharoah) *"Go, serve YHWH your God!"*

(Pharoah) *"YHWH be with you as I mean to let your children go with you!... you menfolk go and serve YHWH, since that is what you are seeking."*

(Pharoah) *"I am guilty before YHWH your God..."*

(Pharoah) *"Go serve YHWH! Only your flocks and herds shall be left behind; your children may go with you."*

(Moses) *"You yourself must provide us with sacrifices and burnt offerings to up to YHWH our God; our own livestock too shall go... not a hoof shall remain behind: for we must select from it for serving YHWH our God; and we shall not know with what we are to serve him until we arrive there."*

Queen Tiye modelled at the time of a sed-feast, near the end of Amenhotep III reign. Some think that she looks unusually sad or perplexed at the relatively sudden major changes at this time.

AKHENATEN'S EARLY REIGN, WHILE STILL AT WASET

Amenhotep III certainly appears to have died suddenly, unexpectedly. His two young sons should both have been ready to take over in top royal roles.

Uniquely, a situation arose that provides one of the key hallmarks of the Exodus saga; his firstborn son, Crown Prince Djhutmose also died mysteriously at about the same time. No cause of death has ever been discovered by examination of his mummy or other archaeological means; he appears to have been a healthy boy in his very young teens and being groomed for a truly top royal future. Only the Bible gives the cause of death. His slightly younger brother, known to us originally only as another Amenhotep, was all but neglected and sidelined as a youth. He had to suddenly take on the role as king, albeit with evident help from his mother Queen Tiye.

So Amenhotep IV was crowned in Waset and there he soon started a building program. He promptly completed the unfinished decoration at the southern entrance to his father's new temple and its pylons, with scenes of himself in worshipping mode.

Likely he will have taken some time to absorb the enormity of his new role and what actions he should take; maybe also he had privately formed some of his own viewpoints as a child, thinking freely as someone who could take an objective and idealistic view of what needed to be done, and what was wrong with his world.

He soon decreed the construction of a huge new temple dedicated to the Aten at Karnak, known as Waset at the time. This temple was called the *Gem (et)-pa-Aten* ("The Aten is found in the estate of the Aten"). Gem-pa-Aten consisted of a series of buildings, including a Palace and a structure called the *Hut-Benben* ('The Mansion of the Benben stone'), which was dedicated to his

wife Queen Nefertiti. He moved quickly once he started; two other great Aten temples were constructed at Karnak at this time, including the *Rud-Menu* ('Sturdy are the Monuments of the Sun Disc Forever') and *Te-ni-Menu* ('Exalted are the Monuments of the Sun Disc Forever')[16]. During this time he did not repress the worship of Amun, and the scorned gods and priests were still active in the fourth year of his reign. The king appears as Amenhotep IV on the tombs of some of the nobles in Waset.

Blocks, called *talatat*, at Gem-pa-Aten were inscribed with expressionistic scenes that broke away from the established artistic tradition and Schlogl[17] explains that the artistic change was 'concomitant with religious change'.

Queen Tiye was likely a huge influence on Akhenaten as well as her previous husband Amenhotep III.

See page 106 for detail regarding her probable role as temporary ruler while Akhenaten was too young to be effective.

The inclusion and surprising prominence and presentation format of the Benben obelisk at *Hwt-bnbn* still has no real explanation. Although the *ben-*

Talatat blocks, originally of uniform size and easily handled for rapid building, from the Gem-pa-Aten temple complex; the first building accomplishments of the new king Akhenaten while still at Waset.

ben stone had generally been linked with sun worship at Heliopolis, it seems that Akhenaten saw in it a quite different symbolism; he may have recognised in it the representation, not of a global Creation action by a now ruined god, but its more likely representation of the birth of Egypt itself, as symbolising the moment of Egypt's creation, after a massive flood, when the sun first glinted on the tip of a mound or hill, and the '*ben-ben*' bird sat on that same tip as the only safe landing place within sight. The celebrant depicted in this huge temple is Nefertiti rather than Akhenaten.[18]

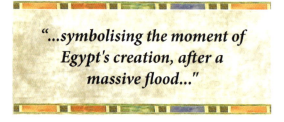

"...symbolising the moment of Egypt's creation, after a massive flood..."

GRADUAL INTRODUCTION OF 'THE ATEN'

How easy was it for Akhenaten to change the nation's religion?

Amenhotep III's main sidekick was another Amenhotep, son of Hapu, a priest of Amun hailing from the Goshen area, and installed directly by Pharoah and not as part of the normal Amun clergy; he could actually bypass these priests by a superior directive from their king.

Also, Anen, who was Tiye's own brother, was installed as a senior priest by Pharoah as 'second prophet' of Amun at Karnak, so it is most unlikely that there was any rebellion or expulsion of Akhenaten by the priests; in fact most of the priests probably gained employment after the big change, in the huge new Aten temples that Akhenaten built not only at Amarna but also whilst still there at Waset. A 'second prophet' is known to have been responsible for the organization of the temple offerings, the cosmogenic sightings, and speaking to the god. This post was taken over by Simut on the death of Anen, around year 30 of Amenhotep III's reign.

One of the first actions of the new king Akhenaten was to impose a new tax on temples and municipalities throughout the land. This tax is known to have demanded silver, gold utensils, bronze (vases), incense, wine and cloth, as well as oil, honey and geese, according to a decree inscribed at the Aten temple at Karnak, and other inscriptions there.[19]

> The number of beneficiaries of the tax is enumerated also in that document: "subordinates of the House of Aten who [are to be supported by these domains, numbering] 6,800 persons, [to whom are assigned] their deliveries for their maintenance [.. which are] to be delivered to the House of Aten [in Upper Egyptian Heliopolis]."

There is also at the time of his third anniversary an amazing diatribe by Akhenaten against the incumbent priests and gods.[19] In part, he declares:

> "Horus ... [their temples] (?) fallen into ruin, [their] bodies (?) shall not ... [since the time of the ancestors (?). It is the ones who are knowledgeable ... Look, I am speaking that I might inform [you concerning] the forms of the gods, I know [their ?] temples [and I am versed in] the writings, the inventories of their primeval bodies [and I have beheld them] as they cease, one after the other, (whether) consisting of any sort of precious stone ... [except for the god who begat] himself by himself, no one knowing the mysteries ... he goes where he pleases and they know not [his] going ... toward him at night. ..."

The key pronouncements here are that the old gods have 'ceased' to be effective and that his new god is quite unique and truly heavenly. This then is an early stage of the development of what became the worship of a sole god, 'the Aten'. Amenhotep IV as he was at that time, proceeded to select useful components of the old pantheon and its iconography until his iconoclasm came to have full strength and he soon saw the need for eliminating not only all carved traces of Amun's presence but even that name as part of his own name, *Amen-Hotep*! It had to go. Akhen-*Aten* would be his new name. That would be in year 5.

His new 'the Aten' with powerful rays had in fact been used previously; Amen-hotep II used it briefly near the Sphinx at Heliopolis; also Thutmose III and Amenhotep III had occasionally used the same device. Akhenaten uses the rays in his second regnal year, in the preparations for the forthcoming jubilee.

Also at this time, we see the start of a new cartouche for the Aten, a double name-ring normally used for kings. Akhenaten would henceforth associate himself closely with the Aten, as his sole representative, as his 'son'.

King 'Tut' (Tutankh-Amun) who was a Pharoah after Akhenaten's reign.

Akhenaten thus gives himself the highest position in the new Aten cult, over-riding the high priest and all other religious leaders who had evidently been morphed into one organisation by the earlier Pharoah Thutmose III, in an as-sertive accession, an ultra-montane move, acceding to the supreme position of all political and religious authority.

He reversed most of the changes that Akhenaten had made.

Amazingly, the only recorded actual dissent comes after Akhenaten's death, almost two decades later, and these records give some idea of how his chang-es were perceived during the Amarna period, and the damage done by the lack of a credible alternative to the ruined gods. The restoration inscription[20] of king Tut, in the Great Hypostyle Hall at Karnak, also a duplicate discovered in foundations of the temple of Montu says in part:

"... all the gods, having repaired what was ruined as a monument lasting to the length of continuity, and having repelled disorder throughout the Two Lands..." *"As for the gods and goddesses who are in this land, their hearts are joyful: the lords of shrines are rejoicing, the shores are shouting praise, and exultation pervades the [entire] land now that good [plans] have come to pass."*

It makes sense that Akhenaten would pick up on Aten as his god, his 'supreme' and sole 'almighty' and 'father ("*itn*"], featured already by his father in likely response to the strong ascendant He-brew influence. Unlike many other gods, Aten had no hard link to a specific place; he was sited centrally and acceptably at Heliopolis with Aper-el as priest, without reference to any original location. Amen-hotep III, in his later years, had made prominent use of Aten[21] (mostly as Aten-Tjehen; 'the dazzling sun disk').

Aten was now gradually featured more prominently, prior to the final declarations by Akhenaten. One of the first detailed expressions is on the tombstone of Suti and Hor, architects for Amenhotep III, in the great 'Hymn for the Aten'[22] now on display in British Museum[23] combining the identities of most other sun gods into the falcon-headed Aten. The actual title of the Hymn is something like *'Adoration of Amun when he rises as Horakhte (Horus of the Horizon)'*:

> *"Hail to thee, beautiful god of every day!*
> *Rising in the morning without ceasing,*
> *[Not] wearied in labour.*
> *When thy rays are visible,*
> *Gold is not considered,*
> *It is not like thy brilliance.*
> *Thou art a craftsman shaping thine own limbs;*
> *Fashioner without being fashioned;*
> *Unique in his qualities, traversing eternity;*
> *Over ways [with] millions under his guidance.*
> *Thy brilliance is like the brilliance of the sky,*
> *Thy colors gleam more than the hues of it.*
> *When thou sailest across the sky all men behold thee,*
> *[Though] thy going is hidden from their sight.*
> *When thou showest thyself at morning every day,*
> *. . . under thy majesty, though the day be brief,*
> *Thou traversest a journey of leagues,*
> *Even millions and hundred-thousands of time.*
> *Every day is under thee.*
> *When thy setting [comes]*
> *The hours of the night hearken to thee likewise.*
> *When thou hast traversed it*
> *There comes no ending to thy labors.*
> *All men, they see by means of thee.*
> *Nor do they finish when thy majesty sets,*
> *[For] thou wakest to rise in the morning,*
> *And thy radiance, it opens the eyes [again].*
> *When thou settest in Manu,*
> *Then they sleep like the dead.*
> *Hail to thee! O disk of day,*
> *Creator of all and giver of their sustenance,*
> *Great Falcon, brilliantly plumaged,*
> *Brought forth to raise himself on high of himself,*

Self-generator, without being born.

First-born Falcon in the midst of the sky,

To whom jubilation is made at his rising and his setting likewise.

Fashioner of the produce of the soil,

....

A mother, profitable to gods and men,

A craftsman of experience, . . .

Valiant herdman who drives his cattle,

Their refuge and giver of their sustenance,

Who passes by, running the course of Khepri,

Who determines his own birth,

Exalting his beauty in the body of Nut,

Illuminating the Two Lands with his disk,

The primordial being, who himself made himself;

Who beholds that which he has made,

Sole lord taking captive all lands every day,

As one beholding them that walk therein;

Shining in the sky [a being as the sun]

He makes the seasons by the months,

Heat when he desires,

Cold when he desires.

He makes the limbs to languish

When he enfolds them,

Every land is in rejoicing

At his rising every day, in order to praise him."

You can see the retention at this stage of reference to the falcon, Nut, Khepri and Amun.   Extended though is the domain of the Aten, now deemed to be over all the earth rather than Egypt alone. It would not be very long though before Akhenaten, thought to be the author of this Hymn, would progress his attempt at theology to the next stage.

Years 5-9 saw the destruction of almost all remote gods in all places now that a replacement was reasonably settled. People whose name included a recognition of 'Amun' were expected to change to the acceptable 'Aten', and of course the young new king Amen-Hotep led the way by changing his own name to Akhen-*Aten*, doing the same with any of his immediate family.

The noted Egyptologist Donald B Redford[24] says, in part:

> "Everywhere, in temples, tombs, statuary, and casual inscriptions, the hieroglyphs for 'Amun' and representations of the god were chiseled out; objects sacred to him were likewise defaced... Osiris and his cycle of mortuary gods suffered a like anathematization. Funerary practices might be spared, but only if purged of all polytheistic elements."

Akhenaten's purge of his father's gods was thorough but not truly complete; he tolerated a low level of 'private' or local gods, and it is important to recognise that he was probably not physically brutal to any people.

King Tut later encapsulates[25] the result of this poorly managed purge, as he surveys the gods in ruins with no effective replacement ever being presented nor adopted in the previous 16 years:

> "... the temples of gods and goddesses from Elephantine as far as the Delta marshes had fallen into ruin, and their shrines become dilapidated. They had turned into mounds overgrown with weeds, and it seemed that their sanctuaries never existed. ... If ever the army was dispatched to the Levant to extend the borders of Egypt, they had no success. If ever one prayed to a god to ask something of him, he never would come at all. ... Their hearts were weakened in their bodies, for they had destroyed what had been made."

In Akhenaten's 5th regnal year he declared that the Aten would no longer tolerate the existence of any other gods[26] and the priesthoods of other gods were disbanded and temple-incomes were diverted to the-Aten.

Stelae-X and M[27] from Amarna, inscribed in his 5th regnal year, are significantly more direct and claim that the revenue of the entire land now belongs to the Aten. Quirke[28] explains the massive impact that all temples had on the socioeconomic fabric of Egypt, as well as on 'its client the royal court', and by taking total control of resources in a cash-less society Akhenaten had effectively ceased exclusive control by coup-de-maître on the fabric of Amun-Ra.

His closest advisor Parennefer (or Wennefer), strongly supported the implementation of the new 'Aten' worship. An inscription on his tomb reads:

> "Now the Sun knows which is the servant that is diligent with respect to offerings. The servant who is not diligent with respect to the offerings of the Aten gives himself over into thy [the king's] power; for the grain imposts of every other god are measured merely in small amounts, but for the Aten they are measured in superabundance."

Between the 9th and 12th regnal years the Aten received its final didactic name which eliminated all traces of the old polytheism - 'Life to Ra, ruler of the two horizons, who rejoices in the horizon in his name Ra, the father who is come as the-Aten'.[29]

The removal of your name was tantamount to an eternal death penalty in

Egypt; criminals were convicted and punished partly by the removal of their name, thus condemned to eternal 'damnation.' One of the conspirators of the Harem Conspiracy of Rameses III had his name changed from Mersure (Ra-loves-him) to Mesedsure (Ra-hates him), meaning his true name would be forgotten and he will thus have no afterlife!

Some of the royal court changed their names to remove them from the patronage of other gods and place them under that of the Aten. Yet, even at Amarna itself, some courtiers kept such names as Ahmose ('child of the moon god'), and the sculptor's workshop where the famous Nefertiti bust and other works of royal portraiture were found, is associated with an artist known to have been called Thutmose ('child of Thoth'). An overwhelmingly large number of amulets at Amarna also show that talismans of the household-and-childbirth gods Bes and Taweret, the eye of Horus, and amulets of other traditional deities, were openly worn by its citizens.

During the reign of Amenhotep III, a major new quarry was opened at Gebel Silsila, where huge quantities of sandstone could be extracted, rather than the limestone that had been in common use previously. This was very good timing indeed, for the construction of Akhenaten's four huge new Aten temples at Gem-pa-Aten as well as a whole new warm-coloured city at Amarna, and to start with, a great *benben* monolith at Karnak.

A ship arrives at the new city of Akhet (Amarna), being built on a totally new site during Akhenaten's regnal years 4 and 9.

Amenhotep-IV ('Amun is satisfied') changed his name to Akhenaten ('beneficial to the-Aten')[30] by his 5th regnal year and the Aten was given a royal titulary and its name was written within cartouches like a royal titulary. About the same time a new residence for the-Aten and the court, untainted by any previous association with the old gods, was established midway between Waset and Memphis with the name Akhet-Aten ('Horizon of the-Aten')[31]

EXCEPTIONAL SED-FEAST TIMING

At Gem-pa-Aten there was only scant presence of the old gods; a relief shows the priests bearing their individual standards of their gods, with the associated caption 'the gods upon their standards' yet there is virtually no activity involving these gods, especially Osiris, Amun, Ptah and Thoth who are all 'conspicuous by their absence.'[32]   All worship is now being turned toward the Aten, this feast being on just the third anniversary of Akhenaten's accession, and likely being prepared during his second year.

Another significant feature is the absence of actual names of dignitaries, quite unlike the prototype previous feasts of Amenhotep where these nobles, priests or similar would have their names etched into the reliefs. The titles are now featured, but not the holders of these titles.[33] A major change in personnel was evidently about to be implemented!

There was however an abundance of bouza, beef and bread, so a good time was likely had by all!

Another unique feature of these rapidly improvised Akhenaten feasts was the prominence given to Nefertiti, even to her depiction in a head-smiting scene! Maybe this was quite intentionally a new consideration for the benefit of the female population.

Amenhotep's vizier Aper-El was retained by Akhenaten and continued his role into the Amarna days.

Akhenaten sought virgin land for his new city of Amarna, land that 'belonged to no god or goddess and no lord or mistress, and no other person has the right to upon it as the owner', according to Paul Johnson in *The Civilization of Ancient Egypt*. He found such a place on a strip along the Nile in Middle Egypt halfway between the political capital Waset and the traditional capital Memphis, an area surrounded on three sides with mountains and on the west with fertile land along the Niles river. He relocated his extended family, loyal nobility, and 20,000 of his subjects to the new capital, which he called Akhet-Aten, 'place where the Aten is effective', or 'horizon of the sun'.

Amarna's temples were open to the sky so the rays of the great sun could blaze down upon the worshippers. In these temples, Akhenaten performed new rituals and ceremonies for his new god. Akhenaten's rituals no doubt included hymns.

ORDER OF EVENTS

Before the Ten Plagues

(from about 1900 BCE) 1st mention of Egypt is Genesis 12:14 with Abram and Hagar (his Egyptian wife).

Joseph captured and taken as slave into Egypt. (Genesis 37)

Pharoah ('king') Amenhotep II (?) "the listener" rules, at time of Joseph.

Waterway and Fayum Basin ('the waterway of Joseph') constructed before time of famine. Government come to own all property, temporarily. Authority of 'nomes' is diminished.

A new king comes to power in Egypt who 'did not know Joseph.' (Exodus 1:8)

This king orders the death of all newborn Hebrew boys. (Exodus 1:22)

Moses is born into this regime. (Exodus 2:2)

Moses is adopted by the Pharaoh's daughter. (Exodus 2:5)

Moses grows up, murders an Egyptian, and flees the country. (Exodus 2:12,15)

Moses marries Zipporah and they have a son. (Exodus 2:12,15)

Eventually, 'in the course of those many days', the king of Egypt dies. (Exodus 2:23)

The Hebrews reside mainly at Goshen/Rameses/Pithon/Delta areas but many will likely have been servants or living in other areas also.

God meets Moses and sends him to the new Pharaoh. (Exodus 3: and 4:)

Moses is 80 years old when he stands before the new Pharaoh. (Exodus 7:7)

The *Bible* indicates that the same Pharaoh whose daughter adopted three-month-old Moses died when Moses was nearly 80 years old! This Pharaoh must have reigned for a very long time.

Reign of Amenhotep III

18th Dynasty: traditionally accepted to be 1570 - 1293 BCE but with many alternative chronologies.[34]

Amenhotep III based at Memphis; had Ptah, creator of the gods as a primary god there.

Amenhotep III, regnal **year 11**: Aten (*Aten-Tjehen* ; Dazzling Sun-Disk) first encountered in a lake scarab inscription on his royal barque. Construction of a massive new royal residence at Malkata, on the West bank at Waset, began around year 11 of his reign and continued until he moved there around **year 29**. The palace was named 'Palace of the Dazzling Aten', also known as 'House of Rejoicing'.

Amenhotep III **Year 30**: his first Jubilee or sed-feast; hundreds of Sekhmet scary black statues made in advance of it; also serpents, rams, lions, jackals, and falcons. The 'third pylon' at Karnak is built, featuring Amun.

Amenhotep III had three Jubilees in **years 30, 34 and 37**, making great efforts to do so authentically according to ancient tradition, especially featuring the resurrection god Sokar. He toured many other towns to re-enact his sed-feast. There hadn't been a sed-feast for very long time prior to his reign. Sekhmet (war, and healing) and Mut ('mother' goddess of primordial waters) were also particularly prominent gods. Also built temples in the Waset, Karnak, Luxor areas.

Amenhotep III third sed-feast in **year 37**: raised Djed pillar as part of the old rejuvenation ceremony; running, shooting, and tossing the caber.

His firstborn son died mysteriously at young age.

Amenhotep III died probably in his **38th regnal year**. He was still building the 'colonnade hall' at the Luxor temple of Amun-Ra at time of death; the decoration of It was continued and modified by Akhenaten.

Reign of Amenhotep IV · Akhenaten

Akhenaten, the second-born son, took over the throne whilst still young, and his mother Tiye evidently supervised for a while.

The 'Long Hymn' inscribed on the tomb of twins Suti and Hor, who had been architects to Amenhotep III, probably written by Akhenaten: *"O sole god, whose powers no other possesses; thou didst create the world according to thy heart, whilst thou was alone."*

Akhenaten's **regnal Year 1**: harangue at start of reign; he specifically says to his courtiers that stone idols are of no value; the third pylon at Karnak is modified by him, featuring an image of Akhenaten being presented to Amun with the inscription *"I rule by his agreement; I join with his strength; I take possession of his power."* Akhenaten carries out more completion and decoration works on his father's unfinished reliefs there.

Naphurureya is the old Akkadian version of Akhenaten's throne name Neferkheperure, as used on a Tushratta letter which expresses sorrow at the news of the recent death of the previous Pharoah. This has been dated now to 'year 2'.

A new word is used for god; '[the] Aten' is different from the old Egypt word NETER (god); demonstrating that god is not physical, but powerful, with a more spiritual presence, and no need of a 'multiple god' classification.

Akhenaten built four new temples at Waset, all for the Aten; gradually used the new 'sun-ray' motif; these huge new temples must have been like skyscrapers blotting out small shops in a city. One of them re-used an old disused palace site.

An impressive open-style shrine is erected at Karnak, using a new fast brick 'talatat' method, involving many people; many old gods retain a mention in it. An unprecedented *sed-feast* is planned by Akhenaten in only his first three years. 'The Aten' is now uniquely given a cartouche like a human king and new identity with rays and hands instead of the old falcon-head.

Akhenaten commissions other works at one of his new towns, Sesebi (Nubia) and also at Memphis. He also built an Aten temple in the south at Kawa ('Gem-Aten'), involving local people in construction at an existing town. The priests at the new temples appear to have been re-employed from old discredited temples; the priests ultimately received the huge number of regular offerings after they were 'accepted' by the Aten's rays and the king.

His closest advisor Parennefer is appointed early on to be Akhenaten's new High Priest of Amun, and strongly supports the implementation of the new 'Aten' worship. His tomb inscription shows that he threatened everyone with inadequate grain supplies if they did not conform.

3rd Anniversary: the likely timing of his first *sed-feast*.

Year 4: Boundary building started at Amarna; Amun still recognised.

Year 5: Amenhotep IV changes his name to Akhenaten, bans all other gods. Akhet-Aten (Amarna) commissioned with the first wave of boundary proclamations.

Year 6: Akhenaten moves to Amarna. Renewal of boundary vows.

Year 7: Son Tutankh-Aten (later Tutankh-Amun) born at Amarna.

Year 9: Amarna now becomes the base for the entire royal court. All the disgraced god-images and references to multiple 'gods' are defaced by a newly commissioned workforce and the temples are closed down or destroyed. Destroying a god name was deemed as 'killing' it for all eternity. Probably another great *sed-feast* at Amarna. He changes his title from 'The Good God' to 'The Good Ruler'.

Year 10: Amarna door lintel produced with memorial to Amenhotep III and family.

Year 12: Probably another great *sed-feast* at Amarna, with foreign envoys.

Year 13: Nefertiti not known from this year on.

Year 14: Queen Tiye dies?

Year 17: Akhenaten dies, and religion later reverts to the old gods under the management of Tutankh-Amun (who changes his name from Tutankh-Aten)

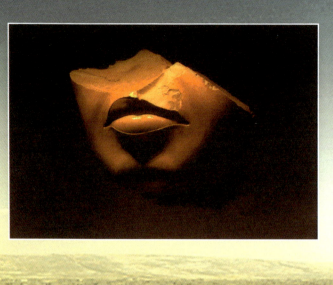

Top:

Yellow jasper statue fragment of Nefertiti, the beautiful wife of Akhenaten

Centre:

Court ladies at an Amarna ceremony

Bottom:

Chariots with Court ladies at Amarna

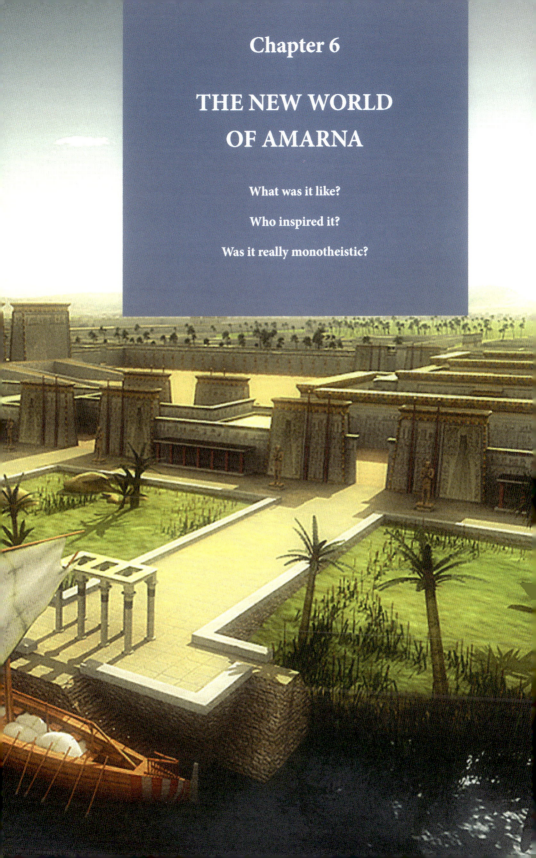

Chapter 6

THE NEW WORLD
OF AMARNA

What was it like?

Who inspired it?

Was it really monotheistic?

WHILST STILL based at Waset, a newly crowned Akhenaten held a surprise jubilee, just three years into his reign, as a young man. This was highly unusual; his father had waited the traditional 30 years for his first one. We can postulate that the spirit of the people needed lifting after the loss of so many of their fighters and senior people.

People must have lost faith in Amun(ism), to enable Akhenaten to bring such an unprecedented and massive change, affecting the deepest thoughts and loyalties of the people, yet without an evident struggle or rebellion: this was a monumental convulsion in society, with what must have been thousands of exceedingly bitter, bewildered, and yet strangely obedient subjects.

The worst sign of any rebellious speech seems to have come from some priests, who must have bad-mouthed him publicly many times; Akhenaten tells in the first Amarna boundary stelae of many 'evil words' in years one, four and five especially, comparing them with other notable great 'evils' spoken in earlier times under Amenhotep III and Thutmosis IV. Of course, they were very angry: most of them likely lost their employment and livelihood, at least for a while.

This early Jubilee is attested on many inscriptions including a depiction of a 'window of appearance' *(see picture on opposite page)* where some gifts are being tossed into the crowd, although the gifts do not appear as plentiful as in later depictions of the royal window at Amarna.

Somehow Akhenaten would have to re-shape the religious beliefs of his remaining people, retaining something of a recognisable old order in the name of a familiar god, the Aten, but gradually introducing powerful new concepts that attempted to explain what they had all been through.

Akhenaten was depicted in what is thought to be an intentionally realistic and unflattering manner.

Some of these fresh Aten concepts may have come from older Suryan traditions and motifs (Aryan, Indian, Syrian—possibly via the Mitanni princesses), with radiating lines of powerful sunshine on some of their iconography.

Another possible influence could have been the old Hindu god Varuna with its slogan of 'truth & order'. Many influences certainly came from Babylon, the Kassites, Aryans and the Assyrians.

There must have been terrible turmoil in Akhenaten's mind; his legacy and memory of a great father, recently deified as Amun; his needing to hold onto ancestral piety, yet realising that there had been no real power in their old gods.

The material culture which is our only legacy of his religion provides a tantalising glimpse at a populist (for a while) takeover by this king who was something of an outsider, supported by his bewildered population rather than the elite priests, nobles and military which had been their lot for centuries. He was undoubtedly sincere in his radical ideologies and made a very bold attempt at Amarna at involving the people in what he saw as a higher plane of

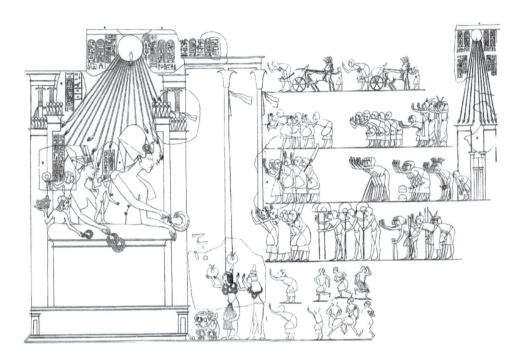

spirituality, albeit with a gratifying surfeit of open-air feasting and communal pleasantness at the thousands of offering tables he provided.

Whatever the stimulus was in the crises at Waset, he evidently felt incredibly driven to make stupendous political and religious changes rather than taking up what probably could have been an easy and exceptionally pleasant reclusive life for him and his beautiful wife Nefertiti.

Boundary stones at Amarna include this telling pronouncement: *"my oath of Truth, which is my desire to pronounce, and of which I will not say 'It is false' eternally forever."* Also, many Amarna nobles honour Akhenaten for his 'Truth' *('Maat')* as opposed to falsehood.

Depiction of the 'window of appearance' at Amarna, with the royals giving small gifts of honour to Ay and his wife as well as other workers.

We should note here again that the name 'Amarna' only dates to the 18th century CE; it was not a 'Tel' or mound either: it was just a riverside desert plain. It was evidently named as Amarna after a local tribe with a similar name, identifying the ancient ruins being re-discovered at that time.

Right:

The hands of Akhenaten and Nefertiti, from an Amarna statue.

WHAT WAS IT LIKE AT AMARNA?

Paradise! – a totally new start, with the emphasis on beauty, light, family life and apparent openness and freedom!

Trade continued in cedarwood, boxwood, diorite, gold, copper, silver, porphyry, marble, ivory, glass, alabaster – and grand villas of nobles were built, with lovely gardens, pools, and a profusion of flowers; there seems to be a certain Minoan influence in the art.

The 'plebs' had their small new houses rather like the subsidised estate homes of modern times.

Amarna palaces had glorious painted floors, walls and pillars, with lotus flowers real and painted, monkeys, young girls, and bright feature decoration. There's a definite feminine feel to the whole place, and far less visible religion. Everywhere there is the joyful sound of construction and at least superficial happiness and music.

It is tempting to draw an inspirational parallel with the William Morris *'News from Nowhere'* [1], a Utopian world with no advertising nor money; arts and crafts abound, and social equality the norm. But with no higher morality or agreed standards to enforce it or make it work, it was doomed to failure; and in real life, Morris became a disillusioned socialist abandoning his own great energies in attempting to achieve a fairer world.

Amarna's temples were uniquely open to the strong sun; one of the Amarna letters hints at how silly this was – what painful worship!

Akhenaten's huge new palace had no less than 542 pillars, and lovely painted pavements. He seems to have had privileged access to his god's *Maru-Aten* (a garden of pleasure, a royal paradise, with a small lake) at southern end of Amarna.

There were very large Police barracks, with head man Mahu in charge of civil order. Most of the Amarna reliefs we see actually depict civil and ceremonial situations, with almost no active soldiers shown. A surprisingly high percentage of women is also notable in the reliefs, in many different contexts.

Key personnel are mostly new, probably inexperienced men.

"Most faces are new, the "old guard" being largely absent" [2] says Don Redford.

Maya, a new army General, *"whom the king made great because of his fine qualities... the only useful one in his lord's opinion, one whom he discerned as a good executive."* [3]

However, Ay was the king's main man; he came from Waset where he had been in office, and was possibly Amenhotep III's brother-in-law. He actually became king later, after King Tut, and he never truly converted to Aten worship. Strange that he survived the total wipe-out of the Exodus military, but maybe as a 'royal' he was privileged to stay in the office and monitor the spare horses.

Some wine jars evidently came to Amarna from Waset, presumably full! They have labels on them indicating "Years 17", "28", "30" of Amenhotep III's reign.

The physical setting out of Amarna reflects considerable thought in terms of symbolism, as well as geometry and alignment. Other writers have explained in some detail the lay-lines, the angles of the rays on some stelae, the alignment of temples, and subtle, divine patterns. The original name of Amarna, 'Akhet' means 'Horizon' (the final phase of the sun just before its re-birth at dawn), thus indicating an intent on maximising the respect for the nameless but powerful 'Aten'; Aten is not actually a name, but is THE aten ('disc', a representation of the sun disc, with its awesome power).

Material tribute was still apparently paid into Akhenaten's coffers in year 12, from 'Syria' (according to an extensive relief on the tomb of Huya, and a similar inscription on the tomb of Meryre); whether this commemmorates an actual festival in that year, or has some other purpose, is not certain, as Huya was generally based in Ethiopia. Whatever its intended purpose, it would no doubt encourage other states to maintain their supplies of tribute despite the evident lack of recriprocal gifts from the new Amarna government.

One notably novel feature of Amarnan royal life seems to be a much greater featuring of family scenes, quite remarkably unlike any previous Pharaonic depictions.

Fragment from Amarna showing hands in adoration of The Aten cartouche

It may be significant that the Israelites, at least in later times, had 11 words for 'children' or 'youth'; they have always been noted to be far more family-oriented than any other ancient peoples. Akhenaten may have recognised this difference, and he seems to be something of an Egyptian trendsetter in featuring his own close loving family in this Amarna period.

One troubling find, though, in the tombs of Amarna, is the huge number of child slaves buried there, evidently dying between ages seven and twenty-five - mostly less than fifteen. All have terrible injuries reflecting their exceptionally hard labour. Possibly 2,000 child bodies are buried there in the roughly dug North Cemetery.

'LIVING IN TRUTH!'

How appropriate it was that the slogan for the new religion was "Living in Truth", and the new capital called "The Aten Is Found", especially in view of the likely disorientation of the people's faith after the Exodus and Plagues. Akhenaten himself seems to typify *'Shu'* (truth) whilst Nefertiti typifies *'Neb'* (sky-mother).

Why did Akhenaten force his people to recognise that there is just one powerful god instead of the hundreds of inert gods they previously had?

There is also a new Truth in their art; a new honesty, even depicting the king with a more unflattering and maybe authentic flaccid, long face, and showing the wrong awkward but realistic poses for trainee soldiers, rather than the proud and artificial authorised poses one may expect.

The Canaan peoples, in contrast, were known to be frequent liars, or at least to put a great deal of 'spin' on their accounts!

Note the hands at the ends of the rays; also the focus on the power and effect of the sun rather than its identity or name.

Religiously and militarily, Akhenaten seems to show an honesty quite unlike previous Egyptian kings; he had already lost massively to the Hebrews, who were now somewhere in the Canaan area... why risk more death and shame? He was truthful with himself and his people, refusing to go after them again. He must have respected their God and the likely success they would have had in any further skirmishes.

Methods of changing people's viewpoints:

Writing & Art. An example of this was the life and works of John Ruskin, whose great influence inspired the Pre-Raphaelites in their art, and the great Arts & Crafts movement of the mid 19th century and beyond. Gone were the dark religious paintings of earlier years, and in came a truth-loving detailed appreciation of romance and nature.

Reformation. Brave leaders put their lives on the line in protesting against abuses by the then established church; they especially changed practices such as indulgences, and the denial of the Bible in local languages. John Hus, Tyndale, Wycliffe, Latimer and Mortimer, Luther were just some who achieved this, and inspired half the world.

Murder. Through the 'dark' ages, enforcement of a particular set of beliefs was achieved by massacre, crusades, burnings, murder, war, and physical persecution.

Name change. St. Petersburg was changed to Petrograd (Peter's City) during WW1 by the Tsar to sound less German, and then later to Leningrad to build favour for Lenin. Stalingrad was renamed to honor Stalin in 1925 when he claimed to have played a major role in defending it, and then it changed to Volgograd when memory of Stalin was sour. The British royals also changed their family name at the start of WW1 to reduce negative attitudes for their German heritage and family connections. Also, at the start of the 21st century, the perception that there was a new 'caliphate' in the Middle East excited many Muslims to take up arms or be radicalised for what they thought could be a bright new start.

Zealous leadership and example. King Josiah, in the Bible, had outstanding zeal for truth and true worship, from a young age, probably being only about 19 when he cleaned up the policies of the government, and set an excellent public example in his own life. Uzziah also had similar zeal, though young, being influenced by a much older Zechariah.

Colour. Attitudes and perceptions, and assocation of ideas can be subtly influenced by the use of specific colours, from exciting reds, authoritative blues, dirty browns.

Typography. Respect, excitement, and ethnic connections are just some of the attitudes that can be affected by the use of appropriate typefaces especially in product branding. Music, poetry & prose. Deep change can be achieved by these artistic expressions.

Personal instruction and mentoring. Using a mixture of reasoning, reading and meditation, even hardened criminals can be transformed into good citizens.

Great speeches. Martin Luther King is an example of this, in revolutionising the attitudes of society with regard to race hatred, and equal opportunity.

Love and affection. The greatest power.

WHAT INSPIRED AKHENATEN TO GO MONOTHEISTIC?

Egypt's old priests appear to have been corrupt and ineffective, taking much of the imported wealth and tribute through a system established, refined and modified during recent centuries; we note that inscription by Akhenaten on a couple of boundary stelae at Amarna;

> *"... priests, more evil are they than those things which I have heard unto year 4, more evil are they than those things which I have heard in the year... more evil are they than...   that the king ... heard, more evil are they than which Menkheperura heard... in the mouth of negroes, in the mouth of any people."*

The Aten was given his first new temple by Akhenaten at Eastern Karnak, right under the noses of these corrupt Amun priests; (rather like a shiny new mosque being built right opposite St.Johns parish church, and financed by the King, on a prime patch of land!)

Amenhotep III had already built his new palace in his year 11; his royal barge *Tehen-Aten* meaning "the sun disk gleams" accompanied a huge water festival when completed (this was the first official use of 'Aten' on an inscription).

Featured there was a unique monolith of the old-style Aten, pictured[4] as the falcon-headed Horus, with his inscribed name *'Horus of the Horizon, rejoicing in his horizon, in his name Shu-who-is-in-the-Aten'* (but with Akhenaten's name on it! – his name had been scribed *over* Amenhotep III's name] – confused? No doubt the Egyptian populace were too!

Maybe something already seemed wrong, at least to a very young Akhenaten, and maybe to others, when a new trend appeared of amalgamating some of the gods. How could this happen to 'gods'? Children often see an objective view of things, a simple overview and summing of a situation, having no vested interest or prejudices to constrain them from an honest appraisal.

The Semitic influence

As previously stated, a much stronger religious influence, a stronger likelihood of monotheistic belief, would be any of the Hebrews who were said to be *"held in high esteem"* by the royal family and many of the people. This would include Moses himself, also his brother Aaron, both of whom were priestly Levites, and all their immediate family, as we know that Moses sister was on an approved speaking level with Pharoah's daughter (Ex 2:3-10), and Moses' own Hebrew mother Jochebed actually brought him up within Pharoah's household, with the full knowledge of the royal daughter. Yet that daughter viewed Moses as her own son.

The mightiest Semite in Egypt was Joseph of course, and ancient historians do link Joseph with the royal family, in a match with the *Bible*.

Here's what Syncellus (quoted in Manetho) said about Joseph's appearance in Egypt: (in paraphrase)

> *"In the Book of Sothis it gives the specific time when Joseph rose to power under Hyksos king, Aphophis, who ruled 61 years. It says: 'Some say that this king (Aphophis) was at first called Pharaoh, and that in the 4th year of his kingship Joseph came as a slave into Egypt. He appointed Joseph lord of Egypt and all his kingdom in the 17th year of his rule, having learned from him the interpretation of the dreams and having thus proved his divine wisdom.' "*

Also, Josephus, the 1st century Jewish-Roman historian, quotes from native Egyptian commentator Manetho (3rd century BCE) and refers to Joseph as Osar-Seph ('Vizier Seph') who in the time of Amenhotep III *"prohibited the worship of the many Egyptian gods"*.

In manhood, Moses was married to Zipporah, and they had sons including Gershom. These are recorded as knowing the actions of the Pharoah when Moses was 60, that is 20 years before the Exodus.

Even some lowly Hebrews, mostly slaves at this time, could have influenced some Egyptian neighbours or even god-toting royals to see an alternative view of heavenly matters.

Consider other examples in the Scriptures, of the little Hebrew girl who years later had the courage to suggest to Naaman, a royal Assyrian that he considers the power of the Hebrew god in ridding himself of leprosy. After initial scepticism, he successfully does that, and he acknowledges the greater power of YHWH.

Then there was Nebuchadnezzar, that great Babylonian king, who ate humble pie (well, grass actually) when he recognised the powerful God who had brought him low for a while.

Similarly, Samuel[5] successfully convinced the Hebrews to abandon their gods; highlighting a benefit in blessings to them after they had a rough time.

Egypt's 'viziers' and other royals

Queen Tiye's origin was not a royal one; she possibly hailed from Mitanni. Also Amenhotep's additional wife Gilukhipa came with 317 handmaids, along with her niece (Tushratta's daughter) – it is thought she could be Nefertiti – all fabulous beauties of Syrian appearance. Amenhotep III was half Mitanni too – his mother was a Mitanni. Amenhotep III was notably more 'normal' than previous Pharoahs, married to a commoner, and more active in sports.

The second wife of Amenhotep III (another of Tushratta's daughters) Tadukhipa was also an outside influence; she was also re-married to Akhenaten, as part of his royal Harem.

Amenhotep III also had Babylonian king Kadashman's sister and also his daughter as additional wives.

Many scholars are of the opinion that Akhenaten's mother, Tiye (pronounced 'tee') who had also been the chief wife of Amenhotep III, and the daughter of Tjuyu (Tuya) was a likely strong influence on Akhenaten's monotheism. These scholars take the popular view that Tjuyu and Yuya were Semitic, thus likely of Hebrew (monotheistic) origin. The Amarna letter EA26 indicates that Tiye must have been an active 'Queen' in her own right for a short time as the mother of the new young king Akhenaten whilst he rapidly adjusted himself to the royal hot seat.

These family links are plainly stated on commemorative scarabs produced at Amenhotep III's succession, thus (in paraphrase) "the Great King's wife Tiye - the name of her father is Yuya and the name of her mother is Tjuyu".

Significantly, a second home was built by Amenhotep III for his Queen Tiye at the Nile delta fortress city of Sarw, in the land known as Goshen, populated largely by the Hebrews who were mostly slaves in Egypt at that time.

Prime ministers ('viziers', of which there were generally at least two at any one time) included some characters who could possibly have been Semitic, and thus already sympathetic at least to the Hebrew belief in one God, through state contact with Moses, or maybe a monotheistic Queen Tiye.

A unique alabaster statue almost certainly of Queen Tiye was recently found at Luxor.

Alabaster was sourced exclusively from the Amarna area, and she wears the falcon-head version of Aten, giving rise to speculation about Tiye's temporary status as a sole 'de facto' Queen in Akhenaten's very early years.

Photo credit: Egyptian Ministry of Antiquities

Viziers like Aper-el (his Semitic name literally means 'servant of El') were advising Akhenaten at a very early time in his reign, and effectively gave foreign support to the monotheistic ideology of the Aten. See the writings of Zivie and Gessler-Lohr on excavations at the Saqqara tombs.[5]

What about Yuya?

Some have the opinion that Yuya was in fact the Bible character Joseph.

Josephus, the 1st century Jewish-Roman historian, quotes from native Egyptian commentator Manetho (3rd century BCE) and refers to Joseph as Osar-Seph ('Vizier Seph') who in the time of (probably) Amenhotep III *"prohibited the worship of the many Egyptian gods"*!

The status given to Joseph in the Hebrew *Bible* (Gen 41: 40-45 and 45:8 mostly) does seem to match the titles given to Yuya in his tomb, including *"Deputy of His Majesty in the Chariotry"*, *"Bearer of the Ring of the King of Lower Egypt"*, *"The Wise One"*, *"Favourite of the Good God"*, *"Great Prince"*, *"Great of Love"*, *"Unique Friend"*, *"Beloved of the Lord of the Two Lands"*, *"One Made Great by the Lord"*, *"He Whom the King has made His Double"*, and *"Holy Father of the Lord of the Two Lands"*. Despite not being of the actual royal family, Yuya was buried in the Valley of Kings; this was extremely unusual.

Also, Yuya's appearance hints at a strongly Semitic ethnicity; a prominently bent, large nose especially seems to be an indicator of Jewish genes.

Alternatively though, as the burial of Joseph according to the Hebrew *Bible* does not match that of the known burial rites and detail of Yuya, it could be that Yuya was a very close relative of Joseph's, possibly a son, with similar high office... this may better fit the generation differential also. The coffin of Yuya features several 'pagan' gods, which would have been anathema to Joseph.

Any 'Vizier' could have also been dubbed with similar titles and status, and this position could be granted to anyone the king chose, from the Fifth Dynasty onward.

In harmony with the Hebrew *Bible* account, Yuya would have been "father to Pharoah" when Amenhotep III was less than a teenager at the time of his fathers death and evidently enjoyed time with this surrogate father Yuya. This is evidenced by childhood items belonging to Amenhotep III as well as Sitamun being found in the tomb of Yuya, probably in memory of them all playing together along with their daughter Tiye.

Yuya was a priest of Min and other gods, also his shabti figure in a box is inscribed with this extremely non-Israelite description, "one in honour with Osiris, one favoured by the good god, Yuya, Justified with the great god." The term 'justified' refers to the mythological process shown on the Book of the Dead where the deceased had to prove that they were honorable, with a heart that weighed less than a feather! They could of course buy the correct answer to the test questions, rather like a Dark Ages 'indulgence' with a payment to priests. This proves that Yuya cannot have been Joseph, as he would certainly not have agreed to this apostasy.

The 'Semitic nose' of Yuya gives rise to the theory identifying him as the possible Joseph, despite all the evidence against that theory.

HOW 'MONOTHEISTIC' WAS AKHENATEN?

Orly Goldwasser, in *The Essence of Amarna Monotheism*[6] differentiates between 'Reduced Monotheism' and 'Mature Monotheism', as well as several other 'theisms'.

'Mature Monotheism' she defines as a view where 'god is the one and only', without the simultaneous existence of other actual gods, nor the possibility of this occurring.

'Reduced Monotheism' she defines as a view where a single god is to be worshipped whilst acknowledging the existence of other gods, albeit the 'wrong' gods. Akhenaten, at his most extreme did take this view, that 'there is no-one but him (the Aten)'.

But this gives rise to the question, 'what do we mean by "god"?' As we saw in chapter 5, it can be anything that is worshipped, whether a famous skilled footballer, or a heavenly being. In some cases, the object of veneration may not even realise that he is a 'god' to anyone.

Other writers have postulated that Akhenaten was a 'henotheist', or even an 'atheist'! Akhenaten did not leave us much in the way of explaining his new beliefs; in fact he doesn't seem to have explained them to anyone, either at the time, or for posterity!

A 'henotheist' is defined as 'a believer in and worshipper of a single god while accepting the existence or possible existence of other gods'. Its the 'belief in' which poses the problem; gods may exist in the minds of other worshippers, so they 'exist' in that sense as gods, yet Akhenaten himself quite clearly respected only his one 'true' god. Similar to 'reduced monotheism' then, but acknowledging that the 'other' gods are only in the minds of other believers.

Yet the cartouches of Akhenaten include the names of Horak, Shu, Re, even Hapi, Shay and Rennutet. The plural word 'gods' is avoided though, and was effaced almost everywhere, not just in Amarna. Some gods actually missed the deletion though, probably intentionally; for example Khnum, originally god of water, who was a regional god based not far away at Iunyt in Upper Egypt. These omissions may have been for reasons of politics, sympathies or just oversight. Other gods seem to be viewed as having been absorbed into 'the Aten' to keep their people happy.

Unlike his human father, Akhenaten did not maintain a claim to be god. Later in his time, he ceased claiming the title 'Good God' for himself, and replaced it with 'Good Ruler'.

Goldwasser explains the 'classifier' aspect of heiroglyphics in the Amarna age; that the Egyptians historically had, at various times, three different 'category' or 'superordinate classifier' icons for the word 'god'; these being a seated human, a falcon on a perch, and a pole with flag.

These are all generic terms for 'god(s)' without meaning a specific actual god, as in the boundary stelae. Goldwasser points out, along with Louis Zabkar in the 1954 article *The Theocracy of Amarna and the Doctrine of the Ba*, that the Aten is quite deliberately generally featured in Amarna inscriptions without the superordinate (category) classifier, as though there was now quite definitely no need for a category of gods, as there couldn't be any other real gods other than the Aten. This is seen as quite intentional, not accidental; *"it points to a high awareness of classification, and strengthens the theory that the strict avoidance of classifier was a conscious move."*

Thus the new word *[the] Aten* (for 'god') was different from the old Egypt word *neter* ('god'); it was now seen as *not* physical, but powerful, spiritual, on a level higher than could be represented by an anthropomorphic idol.

Using the *Bible* to sort the matter, see Jeremiah 10:3-16 for a good explanation of the difference between an image (man-made, lifeless, no spirit, a falsehood, unreasoning and stupid) and a real active God.

Akhenaten did pray quite personally to his Aten, just like a modern-day person may do[7];

> *"The great and living Aten … ordaining life, vigorously alive, my Father… my wall of millions of cubits, my reminder of eternity, my witness of what is eternal, who fashions himself with his two hands, whom no craftsman has devised, who is established in rising and setting each day ceaselessly. Whether in heaven or earth, every eye beholds him without … while he fills the land with his rays and makes everyone to live. …"*

Barry Kemp[8] in *Ancient Egypt*, defines 'religion' as *"devoted fidelity"* (to anything).

Whatever we call his religion, it had no lasting power; it was just as empty as the previous religions, and some 17 years later, in the time of Tutenkhamun, his theology was now itself quite shamed, ineffective, impotent, no better than all the other gods – all gods now in ruins!

Tutenkhamun (whose birth name had been Tutenk-Aten, but quickly changed when in power) describes[9] his new policy, on a stela which says (in part);

> *"the temples of the gods and goddesses from Elephantine to the Delta had fallen neglected; the shrines have become desolate, the sanctuaries as though they never were. The gods have turned their backs on this land."*

Other later inscriptions refer to Akhenaten as a *"rebel"*, even *"that criminal"*.

DID THE PEOPLE REALLY AGREE WITH IT?

Divine statuettes and some minor inscriptions also show several old gods retained by the populace, and it is likely that the average Amarna person, literate or otherwise, probably had little or no perception nor understanding of divine matters. In the rest of Egypt it was probably a case of having superficial allegience to whatever national god there may be, and a private one or two as a spiritual insurance policy against various risks and later life, hoping there was a mysterious, even magical, underlying power based on ancient folklore or collective memories. A god is only a 'god' if it has people worshipping it; otherwise its just a powerful spirit, at best, and probably a lifeless object of distraction or pacification.

Egyptian hearts seem always to have been set on the old gods; even in recent years, people could be seen spinning a disk while reading poetry and reciting spells; and a woman rolling over, or clambering over, 3 times, some stones in water, with a circular motion just as the ancient rites established; and a woman jumping over her little charms; other fertility rites with flour cake, candles and a pottery jar may still be occasionally seen; or the shade of a tree with a saint displayed under it; you may also still see Coptics 'weigh' the soul.

> *"Christianity and the Islam of this country are full of the ancient worship, and the sacred animals have all taken service with Muslim saints"* – Lucie Duff Gordon. [Or in full, see Lucie's *"Letters from Egypt"* 1863]

> *"Nominal Christians as well as Muslims are seen worshipping in the same churches, with Amun Ra, the sun-god and serpent-killer, now calling himself Mar Girgis (St. George), and the old Osiris festival is as noisy as ever, under the name of Seyd el Bedawee. The local ceremonies of births and burial are often not Muslim, but ancient Egyptian."*

Some find it puzzling that the new 'Aten' religion did not truly take hold in the hearts of the Egyptian masses; that they held onto their old gods and idols. Thus Akhenaten can be labeled a 'heretic' in the sense that he was not popular or orthodox.

Looking at various times in history though, its possible to see that there is often a gulf between what is in people's 'hearts' and what is in their minds; the Hebrews often turned to Baal despite seeing powerful works by YHWH; they held onto their *teraphim* at home (although one explanation of this is that the *teraphim* were also necessary proof of a family inheritance); in the 'dark ages' many Europeans became nominal Catholics rather than be murdered at Piedmont or elsewhere; modern Egyptians in the 21st century also hold onto ancient rites, fertility rites especially, despite centuries of opposition from monotheist Islam and also the Coptics.

In the case of Akhenaten's presentation of the new 'Aten', the problems were that he introduced it suddenly, without any real explanation or specific theological or historical reasoning, and that the Aten wasn't actually the powerful god that Akhenaten made it out to be. He seems to have been forced into this 'theology' because of a colossal and public failure on the part of the other gods, and attempted to maintain something of an Egyptian 'status quo' for those who hadn't joined the Hebrews as part of the 'mixed multitude'.

WHY IT FAILED

Whether Akhenaten really deeply believed in the Aten as the 'true' god, or strategically tried to emulate the more successful Hebrews with their very active and powerful God, we just cannot know.

He certainly sounded like a sincere believer, in his various hymns and inscriptions. Can he really have thought, though, that the Aten was really the great Creator? The god couldn't even name himself, or change his own name.

Did the Aten say why he had apparently created everything? What process did he use, and what material did he have available? What did he do before he created everything physical? What guidance is he giving his people? What benefit, apart from fierce sunshine? Could he explain why the royals had eternal life but no-one else did? What did he expect from his people? How could Joe Public get a relationship with him? How does he help people in need? Does he have a family, or invisible assistants? Exactly how does he show love? Is he really the god over all countries, and if so why have we fought them? Why did he use a falcon head for 500 years? What use is he, really?!

No wonder that the man in the Amarna street didn't have any faith in this new god; not only were all the answers missing, there was nothing tangible about him to relate to everyday life, any more than the old gods. It was literally hot (and very sunny) air!

HOW WOULD YOU DESCRIBE AKHENATEN AFTER ALL THESE YEARS?

He has been dubbed the *"world's first monotheist"* (which he certainly was not; there were many of these in earlier times); the *"world's first individual"* (hardly! What about Abram, or Joseph?); an *"atheist"* (pardon?); a *"prophet of internationalism"* (yet he was mostly inward looking); a *"heretic"* (that's a subjective view based on your religious views); a *"pacifist"* (no, he just didn't have an army at the time); a *"henotheist"* (no, he powerfully asserted the existence of one powerful god, deleting references to multiple 'gods'); a *"crank"* (this is a very shallow view of him); a *"criminal"* (maybe he did destroy many livelihoods without due notice or compensation, and it could be that he was also responsible for child slavery). In most of his endeavours, however, he was extremely peace-loving and honourable. There was no more barbarity than there had been in the time of Amenhotep II or in the time of Tuthmosis III, when a fort at Nubia with a temple dedicated to Amun was known to be named *"slaughter of the foreigners"*.

Bearing in mind that he had never anticipated being king, he probably developed an early taste for art and culture; this seems very true when considering the sea-change in royal Egyptian style in that period, and subsequently. As we have seen, he also certainly reacted to something monumental that happened to his people and country... almost certainly the Plagues and the Exodus. He probably had little time to plan a greater strategy commensurate with such an upheaval. Very early in his reign, with no direct experience, and young in years, he tried to quell some of the discontent there must have been with recent leadership; discontent with the gods too... where were they? ... and weren't the Royals part of the godheads they viewed so piously?

Immediately he must have seen that he needed to show that he was indeed in control, that Egypt must now take a new direction, something truly radical that reflected recent events. A new temple – four new temples – featuring a real god that although not understood, obviously had the power.

An early Jubilee, or *sed-feast*, would also help; at least it would make a jolly distraction, and provide a platform to physically give something back to the people, at least some trinkets from the 'window of appearance' at Gem-pa-Aten.

He would have to emphasise that the old gods really were useless and a waste of the country's income and resources: endeavor to keep them happy with an amalgam of god names rolled into the 'Truth' of the 'Aten', whilst starting afresh elsewhere, with full control of all aspects of leadership.

Control of course was difficult because of the evident lack of military or civil enforcement resources, hence there seem to be reports of great unrest at that time, at least in most areas far away from the new royal city Amarna.

Without detailed or understandable tenets or doctrine, there was no plerophory among the intended worshippers. The situation was just as confusing for them spiritually as it was before, but in a completely different way. This 'Aten' did not speak to them, hadn't written anything, and probably didn't look like he was making much of an improvement in the land, outside the beautiful, colourful new Amarna.

Many Egyptians had left the land, joining the Hebrews; probably around three million people in total. Families must have been torn apart for some time, and family incomes decimated. Local leadership all but gone. Priests unemployed. Many public or religious buildings damaged, defaced or closed. Fear of rapidly increasing crime and violence, and a radical change in whatever education the children were getting.

Maybe it is fairer to describe him as an intelligent young man, thrust into public service and high office without due training, something of a natural dreamer perhaps, but genuinely god-fearing and trying to rapidly implement a new political strategy that even he didn't quite have full control of. He was undoubtedly poetic, artistic and romantic. As a thinker at that high level, he probably didn't have the appropriate support or time to make full sense of all the changes he was making, and the means to implement them fast enough throughout both Lands.

His new religion was a reaction rather than a planned revolution; in the absence of any liturgy, it was **effectively the worship of Nature**, with all former gods now discredited, and the God of the Hebrews seeming to be unacceptable to the remaining population of Egypt. Note that the *Bible* says that a huge 'mixed company' of Egyptians had in fact gone with the Hebrews, evidently un-invited but accepted just the same, in their trek to their Promised Land.

A sort of religious void existed, in which Akhenaten seems unable to involve the people in any meaningful relationship with his new god, 'the Aten'. They continued to privately relate to their old gods, but went along with offerings at the huge new bright Amarna temple, enjoying a sort of freedom and pleasure which probably had been long absent.

Egyptians had always accepted the idea of multiple deities, with a mysterious 'Great One' hidden behind or within their personal favourites. Only in Amarna were all other deities officially removed, with a ban on darkness and a new focus on light and beauty. The new religion suggested awareness of a common enemy, Amun, on which to pile all the blame for recent and past evil and losses.

A colossal statue of Akhenaten holding the symbols of power, from his Aten Temple at   Karnak. Now in the Egyptian Museum of Cairo.

A comparable action was taken later by Cyrus the Great of Persia, when he gave people their favoured gods and temples back, and made them happy and less likely to rebel or fight again. The *Cyrus Cylinder* testifies to this, as well as Ezra chapter one in the *Bible*.

It wasn't Egypt's priests who directly arranged for the old gods to return to favour in later years, in the time of King Tut; it was Tut's government, although no doubt responding to considerable pressure from the priests as well as the people.

One of several boundary stelae at Amarna, defining the official royal policy in creating the new city.

Three of them cryptically refer to the 'entire army' being 'expelled' with 'many people'.

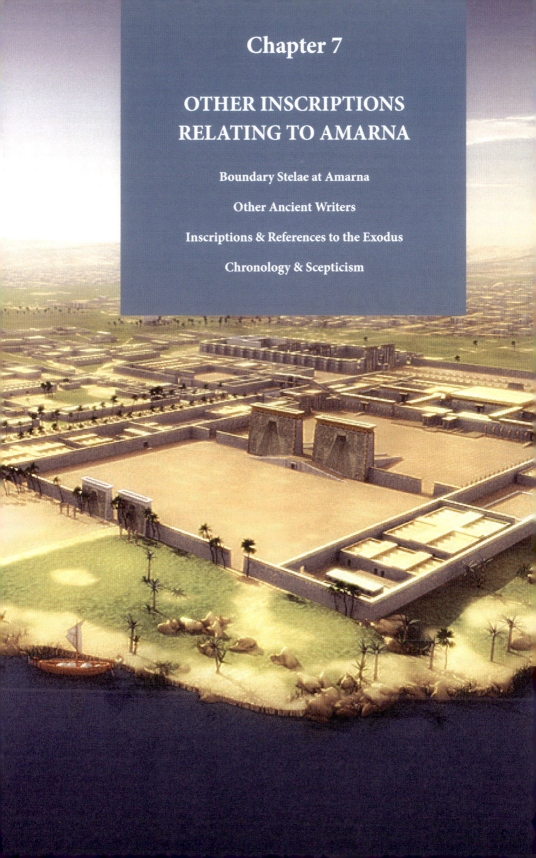

Chapter 7

OTHER INSCRIPTIONS
RELATING TO AMARNA

Boundary Stelae at Amarna

Other Ancient Writers

Inscriptions & References to the Exodus

Chronology & Scepticism

'STELA X' AT AMARNA

"The Amarna Boundary Stelae" [1] by John Johnson (Horus Egyptology Society, at Wigan), p113 (with interlinear on page 76) says that after 384 lines of read-able text on this *'Boundary Stela X'* which was one of the first three stone in-scriptions to be carved at the new city Amarna ('Akhetaten'), chiselled into the north-eastern corner of Amarna in [it actually says] 'Akhenaten's 5th regnal year', there are suddenly (and quite mysteriously!) 20 entire and probably very important lines of text missing, then this cryptic phrase; [at line 385] :

> *"……….. forever and ever. ….the father Ra-Herakhty… and effecting the expulsion of some of the people with the army in its entire … and … arranged at the beginning of…. "*

AND IMMEDIATELY BEFORE IT, line 359 refers to *"offense(s) by gods & god-desses"* to be kept out of Amarna. Is this a reference to the epoch-making of-fenses that caused the Plagues and the Exodus, and subsequently the creation of and move to Amarna? This is how it reads;

> *"I will make the circuit of Aten to be administered… for him and the city similarly stopping … a great offence by any god or goddess against Akhetaten in a document of any god or goddess…"*

or in another translation [1] of the context:

> *"… continually forever … the father, [Hor-Aten] … and effecting the expul-sion [of some group of] people, (with) the army in its entirety. […]s (and) […]s being arranged at the beginning of … with exuberant [rejoicing …] in Akhet-Aten, on behalf of everyone and upon [the king… "*

AND BEFORE THAT, there is a list of who came to Amarna at its creation; yet line 73 mentions no army coming from anywhere. This surely is very sig-nificant, and quite strange in the context of the huge upheaval of men and materials in the move to Amarna, and the mention there of 'ramparts' (line 159) 'boundaries' and previous offensive (line 265) behaviour. All the more strange when you consider the excessively verbose nature of these inscrip-tions, and no mention of the army elsewhere in the decrees, apart from the 'entire' 'expulsion' reference. Remember that 'some of the people' (in fact a great many Egyptians as well as the Hebrews) were 'expelled' from the land after the Plagues, and they could be said to be 'with' the army who chased after them. It doesn't say where they were expelled to; we know that they did not end up in Amarna, though.

Also of significance may be line 73 which lists 'bringing' the 'kings compan-ions' and 'great ones', the 'supervisors of the guard' (not the army), the over-seers of works and the officials of the court'. Intriguing!

Of interest too is the mention (lines 267 - 270) of the offensive words being specifically against 'my father', 'Aten' or 'Re-Herakhty'… what had he done to deserve such words? He talks a great deal about *"my father Aten"* who *"advised*

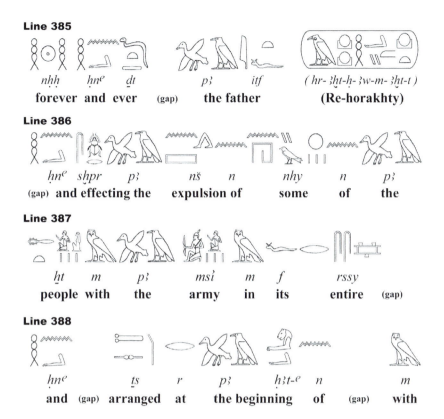

Line 385

nḥḥ   ḥnꜥ   dt   pꜢ   itf   (ḥr- Ꜣḫt-ḥ- Ꜣw-m- Ꜣḫt-t)

forever and ever   (gap)   the father   (Re-horakhty)

Line 386

ḥnꜥ   shpr   pꜢ   nš   n   nhy   n   pꜢ

(gap) and effecting the   expulsion of   some   of   the

Line 387

ḫt   m   pꜢ   msi   m   f   rssy

people with   the   army   in   its   entire   (gap)

Line 388

ḥnꜥ   ts   r   pꜢ   hꜢt-ꜥ   n   m

and   (gap) arranged   at   the beginning   of   (gap)   with

me" to create the new city Amarna; this refers to the god Aten, whom he views as his spiritual 'Father'.

Lines 385-388 of the Stela X at Amarna, mentioning the 'expulsion of the [entire] army' with 'some of the people'.

Incidentally, he says specifically that the previous two Pharoahs were Neb-Maat-Re (Amenhotep III) and prior to that, MenKheprw-Re (Thutmose III).

Could line 386 be referring back to the real reason why Amarna was built, namely the events of the Exodus and preceding 10 Plagues when those catastrophic events EFFECTED (i.e. "made happen") *"the expulsion of some of the people with the army in its entire"...!* Especially in the context of those preceding lines [359] referring to *"offenses by gods and goddesses"*.

It is a pity that those previous 20 lines are missing, worn away or intentionally vandalized, on all three of those contemporary stelae [K, M and X]! *Stela M* is virtually gone entirely.

> *"...effecting the expulsion of ... the army in its entire..."*

SURAT

The 7th Sura deals with the Plagues, and the 20th - 28th Sura (chapter) of the *Qur'an* deals with the Exodus. This is the Arabic variant of the Moses and Exodus account found in the Bible, with some significant differences in detail and emphasis.

THE 'EL-ARISH SHRINE'

The 'el-Arish shrine', made of black granite and discovered on the border of Egypt and modern-day Israel, bears a long hieroglyphic inscription using the same description of the plagues as Exodus 10:22 (with minor differences, and some uncertainty as to translation). This shrine (*naos*) was evidently written in later Ptolemaic times, about a major event from an earlier era...

> *"...the land was in great affliction. Evil fell on this earth...there was a great upheaval in the residence (of the pharaoh)...nobody could leave the palace during nine days, and during these nine days of upheaval, neither men nor gods (ie., the royal family) could see the faces of those beside them."*

It also refers to the Pharaoh's pursuit of the Hebrews whom he followed to Pi-Khiroti, the biblical Pi-Ha-Khiroth, where he was plunged in the "whirlpool." We are informed in Exodus 14:2, 9 of its location, *"between Migdol and the sea, before Baal-Zephon."*

The likely route of the Exodus, based on specific names listed in the Bible book of Exodus

MANETHO & JOSEPHUS

Josephus had many sources, having access at various times to temple records and Roman histories, as well as the most authentic and complete version of the *Pentateuch (Torah)* ever available, actually from Nehemiah's own temple version of it, as well as many other fine ancient sources.

William Whiston[2], the most notable English translator of Josephus works, says *"Josephus must have had much more completer copies of the Pentateuch, or other authentic records now lost, about the birth and actions of Moses, than either our Hebrew, Samaritan, or Greek Bibles afford us."*

He says that Abram took maths & astronomy from Ur to Egypt; this is not mentioned in the Bible, but probably true. Arabic words in mathematics and astronomy support the idea strongly; words like al-gebra, zero, zenith, root, sine.

As a Jewish/Roman historian Josephus quotes the early Egyptian historian Manetho with regard to early Egyptian events. Manetho was a third-century BCE historian and priest of Egypt, who wrote a *"History of Egypt"*. Unfortunately, Manetho is viewed as particularly unreliable and inaccurate, but did make one of the most complete attempts at listing the full history of early Egypt. Josephus quotes him but doesn't trust him. Both are rather muddled in this matter, but there is some value in what is written, nonetheless.

Manetho says that the Exodus Pharoah was 'Amenophis' (the Greek equivalent of Amenhotep), and that he was 'son of Rameses, father of Sethos'. That is where it is rather muddled, but the nearest Amenophis to Rameses or Sethos would be Amenhotep III or Amenhotep IV (Akhenaten), and Josephus mentions that there were in fact two concurrent people with that Pharaonic name.

Josephus records the Exodus as history in his great *'Antiquities of the Jews'*... see paragraph 2:15.2:

> *"They left Egypt in the month Xanthicus (Nisan, in the Israelite calendar), on the fifteenth day of the lunar month; four hundred and thirty years after our forefather Abraham came into Canaan, but two hundred and fifteen years only after Jacob removed into Egypt. (28) It was the eightieth year of the age of Moses, and of that of Aaron three more. They also carried out the bones of Joseph with them, as he had charged his sons to do."*

Josephus says[2] that Moses was also known as Osarsiph (a priest).

Most interestingly, Josephus tells at some length about the actions of the two Amenophis (Amenhotep III and IV) as well as Moses, all concurrent.: Here is a selection of it, from his *Against Apion* 1.26:

> *"Manetho forgets how he had already related that the departure of the shepherds for Jerusalem had been 518 years before, for Thutmosis was king when they went away."*

and then..

> "Amenophis seemed to partake of a divine nature, both as to wisdom and the knowledge of futurities."

> "... he says their number was 80,000, whom he sent to those quarries which are on the east side of the Nile, that they might work in there, and might be separated from the rest of the Egyptians. He says farther, that there were some of the learned priests that were polluted ... but that still Amenophis, the wise man and the prophet, was afraid that the gods would be angry at him ..."

> "... they appointed themselves a ruler out of the priests of Heliopolis, whose name was Osarsiph, and they took their oaths that they would be obedient to him in all things. He then, in the first place, made this law for them, that they should neither worship Egyptian gods..."

> "... his name Osarsiph from Osiris, who was the god of Heliopolis; but that when he was gone over to these people, his name was changed, and he was called Moses."

> "Now, for the first occasion of this fiction, Manetho supposes what is no better than a ridiculous thing; for he says that 'King Amenophis desired to see the gods'. What gods, I pray, did he desire to see? If he meant the gods whom their laws ordained to be worshipped, the ox, the goat, the crocodile, and the baboon, he saw them already; but for the heavenly gods, how could he see them and what should occasion this his desire? To be sure, it was because another king before him had already seen them. He had then been informed what sort of gods they were, and after what manner they have been seen, insomuch that he did not stand in need of any new artifice for obtaining this sight."

> "he saith himself that Amenophis's son had 300,000 men with him, and met them at Pelusium."

> "Cheremon says; for he also, when he pretended to write the Egyptian history, sets down the same name for this king that Manetho did, Amenophis, as also of his son Ramesses..."

> " Cheremon sets down Joseph as driven away at the same time with Moses, who yet died four generations before Moses; which four generations make almost 170 years."

So you can select from that which bits are fact and which fiction or muddle, but there remains a thread of certainty that the Hebrews under Moses did in fact escape from Egypt at the time of an Amenhotep (Amenophis).

Donald B Redford[3] recognized Manetho's 'Osarseph' story as related to the Amarna religious revolution. He says:

> *"... a number of later independent historians, including Manetho, date Moses and the bondage to the Amarna period?"*

Redford[3] also confirms that:

> *"The figure of Osarseph/Moses is clearly modelled on the historic memory of Akhenaten. He is credited with interdicting the worship of all the gods, and in Apion, of championing a form of worship which used open-air temples oriented east, exactly like the Aten temples of Amarna."*

OTHER WRITERS

Eusebius

Eusebius quotes a book by Artapanus, who in turn quotes an unknown ancient work, which tells of the time of plagues, thus, *"hail and earthquake by night, so that those who fled from the earthquake were killed by the hail and those who sought shelter from the hail were destroyed by the earthquake. At that time all the houses fell in and most of the temples."*

Lysimachus

Another ancient writer, he also says that Moses and Joseph were in the Exodus at same time.

Strabo

A pagan historian who was born in 54 BCE also referenced[4] the Exodus: "Among many things believed respecting the temple and inhabitants of Jerusalem, the report most credited is that the Egyptians were the ancestors of the present Jews. An Egyptian priest named Moses, who possessed a portion of the country called Lower Egypt, being dissatisfied with the institutions there, left it and came to Judea with a large body of people who worshipped the Divinity."

Artapanus

Artapanus of Alexandria, from around 3rd century BCE, wrote that Pharoah Palmanothes was ruling when Moses was born, that Pharoah's daughter Merris adopted a Hebrew child whom she called Moses, that Moses led a military campaign against the Ethiopians just as Josephus says in great detail. Artapanus adds that Merris married a later king Khenephres, who ultimately died from elephantiasis.

Some think that Palmanothes is a Greek translation of Amenhotep, and that Khenephres is Neferkheperure (Akhenaten).

The Haggada

The Jewish *Haggada* also refers to the last night of the plagues, when the coffin of Joseph is said to be found lying on the ground, lifted from its grave.

Christian 'Greek' Scripture

Jesus Christ himself, in the Gospels, and the rest of the Christian Scriptures refer to the Exodus as historic over a hundred times. The 'Lord's Evening Meal' is based on the Jewish Passover, with the timing, the unleavened bread and the wine precisely matching it, as well as the unique moon phase being a consistent reminder of the original Passover night in Egypt.

Soleb 'YHWH' Inscription

This earliest known inscription has God's name as YHW (the famous Hebrew tetragrammaton of God's name also includes a final 'h' originally as a vowel) dates back, amazingly, to the reign of Amenhotep III on a temple column base which commemmorates the conquests of various tribes, including possibly *"YHWH in the Shosu land"*, or in other translations[5], *"the Shasu land of YHWH"* or *"land of the Shasu-YHW"*.

See chapter 8 of this book for much more detail on this.

Egyptian Chariot Wheels Found?

While tantalizingly convincing, these reports and photographs, seem to be from the wrong part of the Red Sea, an unusually shallow part of the Gulf of Aqaba. The author does not think that they relate to the Exodus. The recorded route of the Exodus, quite precise in the Bible, may not match.

One of many suggested relics from the sinking of Egyptian 6-spoked military chariots in the Red Sea.

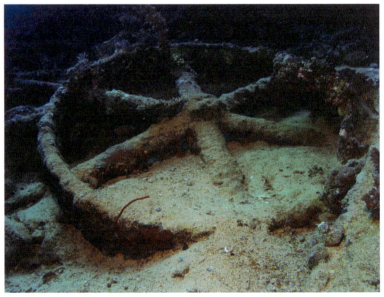

DNA Mummy Tests

iGENEA claimed to have reconstructed the Y-DNA profile of Tutenkh-Amun, his father Akhenaten and his grandfather Amenhotep III . As this is highly contested, it is best ignored for the purpose of this book.

Isaiah Chapter 19

The dating of this ancient writing makes it totally irrelevant to the Exodus, despite some authors claiming otherwise; it is a much later prophecy, and needs no consideration here.

SCEPTICISM

A prime example of the level of scepticism surrounding the Exodus is seen in the words of Israel Finkelstein, who speaks[6] of *"the rise of the true national state in Judah [in the eighth century BC]. . . That national state produced a historical saga so powerful that it led Biblical historians and archaeologists alike to recreate its mythical past—from stones and potsherds."*

Other notable sceptics[7], include Bugliosi, Norma Franklin, Rabbi Wolpe and Mansour Bourak (working with a dig at Luxor) who is on record saying that *"no documented evidence has been found"* other than in the holy books, and other far-out sceptics who say, for example, that there were never any slaves in Egypt.

But lack of evidence is no evidence of lack.

As we've seen, though, there is ample documented evidence from Egyptian and other texts, not only of the certainty of the Exodus but also the huge amount of circumstantial evidence from the two reigns relevant to it.

The reader here can decide whether the huge weight of evidence represented not only by the points in this book but also in particular by the Jewish and Christian histories and traditions which are clearly based on events which were extremely powerful, and the inspired Bible which has so often been doubted but has always proven to be solidly accurate not only in its detailed historical accounts but also, uniquely, in its supernatural prophetic content.

DEBATES ABOUT CHRONOLOGY

The Keeper[8] of the Department of Egyptian Antiquities at the British Museum, T G H James, said this on the incompleteness of Egyptian history:

> "The history of Egypt can be compared with a document of great length, large parts of which are missing, while the preserved portions are rendered imperfect by lacunae, obscure sections and places where the text is difficult to establish with certainty. Sir Alan Gardiner, the most devoted of Egyptologists, who never failed to appreciate the inadequacies of his lifelong field of study, was brutally honest in his verdict on the surviving record: 'What is proudly advertised as Egyptian history is merely a collection of rags and tatters.' What he means - and he makes it quite clear in his subsequent remarks - is that the raw material for the writing of a satisfactory history, covering the whole of the three-thousand-year span, is insufficient and sketchy."

On the reliability, or otherwise, of Egyptian boasts:

> "The desire to record great and glorious deeds is an understandable human weakness, and the ancient Egyptians were no more inclined than others in proclaiming their victories while disguising, or ignoring, their failures. The public statements of their kings and great nobles, confident and vainglorious at the best of times, achieve particular weight and authority when they are inscribed in fine monumental hieroglyphs accompanied by larger-than-life reliefs of dramatic actions on the walls of great temples. How much of the truth do they incorporate? Much, certainly; but in emphasis and interpretation they are often undoubtedly slanted away from reality."

> (p26) "It seems to be generally true that the reliability of an Egyptian historical text depends to a marked extent on the measure of success accompanying the events recorded. The less there is to be ashamed of, the more easily may the truth be recounted."

The whole of T G H James' first chapter, entitled *'The Written Record and its Validity'* is worth a read.

Which Chronology?

The three most painstakingly thorough and complete examinations of the Bible's chronology were arguably those by Bishop Ussher, James Playfair and the International Bible Students who give their Exodus dates as 1493* BCE, 1498** BCE and 1513*** BCE respectively - all within just 20 years of each other.

* This date is shown on the excellent British Museum *'Time Chart of History',* originally published in 1890 as *'Deacon's Synchronological Chart of Universal History',* hand-drawn by Prof Edward Hull and printed on canvas, almost twenty feet long. Re-published later by Studio Editions and still available.

** This date coincides with an alternative theory that Thutmose II was the Exodus Pharoah; Alfred Edersheim proposes this in his *Old Testament Bible History*, based on the fact that he had a brief, prosperous reign and then a sudden collapse with no son to succeed him. Edersheim says that Thutmose II is the only Pharaoh's mummy to display cysts, possible evidence of plagues.

*** This date is calculated backwards from the 'absolute date' of 539 BCE, agreed by virtually all experts, both secular and Biblical, and published in many works.

Recently there has also been much revision of the Exodus date by David Rohl[9] and also Timothy Mahoney[10], resulting in what is termed 'New Chronology'.

Incidentally, the Bible also gives strong indications regarding characters such as Joseph; he was born around 1767 BCE, and was age 110 when he died in or around 1657 BCE. There were many other Hebrew characters also who had very strong connections with the Egyptian royals, and some of these can be dated at least approximately from Bible verses.

Note that we are using the abbreviation BCE, as this is now recognized by the academic world as the correct terminology and reference point rather than the old 'BC'. 'Before the Common Era' retains the dates that have been in use for centuries, while recognizing that Christ was not born in the year zero.

The problem with traditionally accepted Egyptian chronologies is that they are based on several very unreliable or ambiguous sources; as we have seen, Manetho the 3rd century BCE historian, provides a confused, gappy and very unreliable list of kings, with only poor part-copies still existing. The recorded rising of the star Sirius in 'year 9 of Amenhotep I' has been linked tenuously to 1537 BCE, but is questioned. Also, other noted lunar dates are far from being absolute. Too many variables such as reign length, co-regencies, and missing king names, prevent anyone from being really certain.

The Bible does not contradict the memorial monuments left in Canaan during the ensuing 400 years after the Exodus; these monuments commemorate victories by Seti and Rameses within the years covered by the books Joshua and Judges. There are many Bible references to the power of Egypt throughout those years, and the assistance given to various city states.

There were four generations from the time of Jacob's family entering Egypt, through to the Exodus; the Exodus was 215 yrs after Jacob arrived there. These generations are represented by Levi, Kohath, Amram and Moses. When Jacob arrived, Joseph was already there the previous 25 years.

See Exodus 6:16, 18,20 *"These are the names of Levi's sons by their lineage: Gershon, Kohath, and Merari; and the span of Levi's life was 137 years. ... The sons of Kohath: Amram, Izhar, Hebron and Uzziel; and the span of Kohath's life was 133 years. ... Amram took to wife his father's sister Jochebed, and she bore him Aaron and Moses, and the span of Amram's life was 137 years."*

We are here focussing on circumstantial and recorded evidence rather than a single focus on a questionable astronomical sighting and resultant date.

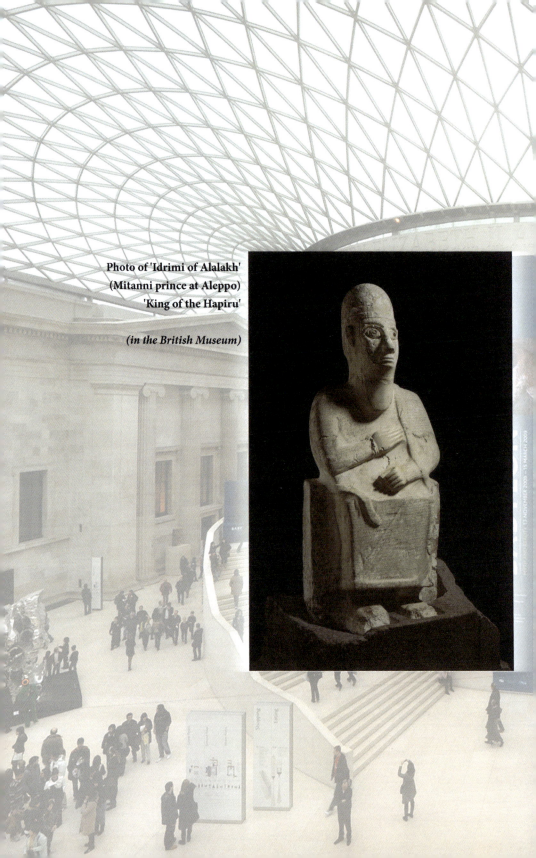

Photo of 'Idrimi of Alalakh'
(Mitanni prince at Aleppo)
'King of the Hapiru'

(in the British Museum)

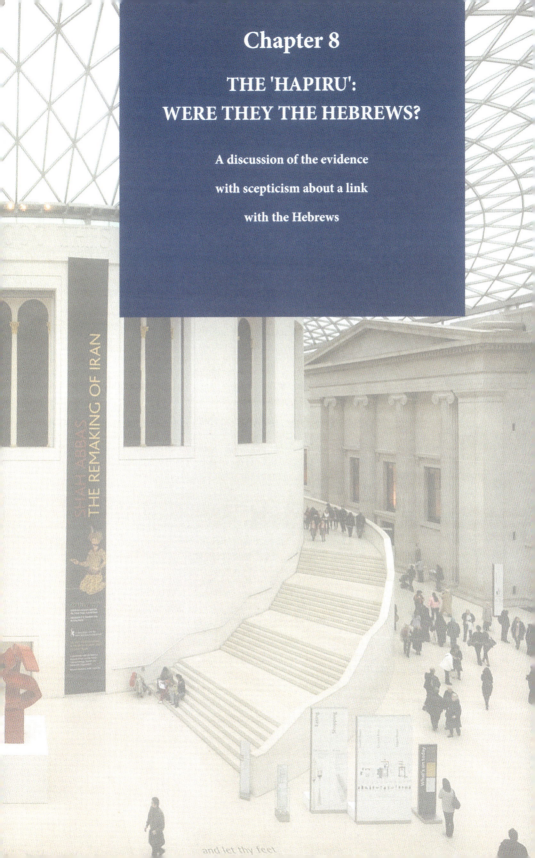

Chapter 8

THE 'HAPIRU': WERE THEY THE HEBREWS?

A discussion of the evidence

with scepticism about a link

with the Hebrews

A TERRIFYING, NOMADIC, MARAUDING and highly successful fighting band of people active throughout the Egypt and Canaan areas around the time of the 18th Dynasty, certainly and tantalisingly sounds like it could have been the Hebrews. Add to that, the similarity of their name variously spelled 'Apiru', 'Hapiru', 'Habiru', and it is even more tempting to make that connection.

The name in Egyptian[1] was spelled 'pr.w which basically means a group of people (thus the "w" suffix) and who are variously described in writings as nomadic or semi-nomadic invaders, raiders or migrant workers. Reference to them stretches across many cultures including Egyptian, Sumerian, Akkadian, Hittite, Mitanni and Ugaritic writings, and goes as far back as at least 1740 BCE and goes beyond the later years after the Hebrews had left Egypt and the Sinai wilderness. In Akkadian writings they are known mostly as *SA.GAZ* but also an equivalent of 'Hapiru' (*'habbatu', plunderer or bandit*), as well as being described as 'soldiers from the West' with mostly Akkadian names, and known for their indiscriminate violence.

However, a closer look at the written detail from various sources shows quite clearly that they cannot have been the Hebrews. They must have been another roaming and more militaristic group, which after all has been quite common throughout the very long history of that region.

The argument for

Even in the Hebrew *Bible*, it refers to the fleeing Hebrews as 'men of war' in Deuteronomy 2:14 as they wandered enroute to Canaan after the Exodus; so who were they fighting? ... and do they fit the timing and descriptions?

The Amarna Letters frequently mention the Hapiru, and describe the almost incredible successes they had in conquering a large number of the Canaanite cities, and in accepting new recruits who voluntarily joined them from other peoples. Their success reads as though they had some kind of invincibility that shocked their target subjects into early and easy submission.

A letter found at Taanach contains the personal name Ahiyami (Ahiyawi?) which in a mis-reading, appears to hint at a connection with Yah (but can also be Ye or Yi). Paton[2] in his *"Israel's Conquest of Canaan"* suggests, *"This favors the theory that the Habiru in Canaan were Israelites".*

W F Albright[3] claims that in Amarna Letter EA 252 by Labayu (at Megiddo) there is an archaic Hebrew proverb. He says almost half of EA 252 is in pure Canaanite (early Hebrew). The text compares with Proverbs 6:6 and 30:25, *"If the ants are smitten, they do not accept quietly, but they bite the hand of the man who smites them"*.

The battle involving the Hapiru at Kadesh (Qadesh) seems to have matching accounts in the *Bible* [Deuteronomy 2:14] as well as in the Amarna Letters [EA 189], where the city was similarly not taken.

The argument against

Most scholars have rejected the identity of the Hapiru with the Hebrews, as the term Hapiru describes a class of people rather than an ethnic group.

The Hapiru are found at widely diverse locations and times around the region, unlike the tightly bound clan of Israelites, thus the term is most unlikely to refer to the Hebrews/Israelites.

The nature of the actions taken by the Hapiru is not a good match with the Hebrews; especially with regard to the accepting of bribes, joining with other forces at a time when they wanted to be exclusive, and military activity well outside their geographical area of interest; for example Byblos mentioned in the Amarna Letters as being attacked by the Hapiru, but this was far beyond the area designated for the new domain of the Israelites.

They spoke no common language[4], had no common ethnic identity, were quite lawless, and had non-Hebrew personal names.

The British Museum has a great statue of Idrimi of Alalakh (a Mitanni prince at Aleppo), who claimed to be a proud 'King of the Habiru'... but of course the Hebrews had no kings until much later.

The Amarna Letters refer to some of the same place names[5] as the Bible, but the names of people and kings are quite different. Jericho is not mentioned at all, yet it has major status in the Bible account. The Amarna Letters have Abdi-Khepa as king of Jerusalem whereas Adoni-zedek is king in the Bible account at Joshua 10:3.

Highlighting the difficulty and potential confusion in grasping the true meaning of such short Egyptian and Akkadian names and words is this image[6] from the inscriptions recording the Battle of Kadesh showing one of the "ibrw" or mounted bowmen used as scouts or messengers by the Egyptians.

"ibr" is the Egyptian word for horse and "w" is the plural suffix.

WHAT ABOUT THE 'SHASU - LAND OF 'JAHU' OR 'YAHWE'?

Another intriguing name found in ancient Egypt is 'Shasu', and 'Land of the Shasu-YHW', or 'Yahwe in the Shosou Land'.

This relates to temples built by Amenhotep III as well as Rameses II in Nubia, notably at Soleb pictured here, and which were in honour of their god Amun-Ra in respect of his perceived superiority over other gods and peoples, including the 'Shasu'.

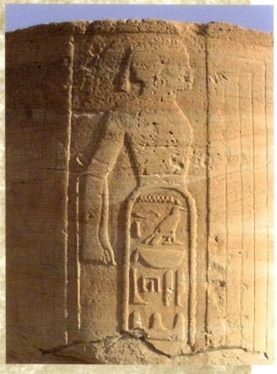

Scholars generally believe that 'Shasu' refers to the nomadic Bedouin, and that 'YHW' refers to a place or district rather than specifically to a god. It is quite possible though that a place name could refer not only to its location but also its adopted god; in fact this was quite common throughout that region.

Thus many peoples who worshipped YHW would have had that connection reflected in the name of the city or 'land' where they lived.

This is only a tenuous and supposed interpretation of it though, and may merely be a similarity of name.

The use of YHWh

The great significance of these inscriptions is two-fold; firstly, that the real name of the great Creator, the Hebrew God YHWh could be seen in these several heiroglyphic texts, and secondly that the one at Soleb in Nubia dates to the reign of Amenhotep III, as it was his temple.

Thus, together with the accuracy of the Bible, it can be proved that Amenhotep III had knowledge of this sacred Name of the Hebrew God, and makes full sense of the Biblical reference to that Pharoah's using the actual name in his dialogue with Moses.

The Pharoah clearly knew of the Name, but was evidently far too haughty to accept the status of such a power, until it was demonstrated by means of the Plagues and finally the Exodus.

The use of the actual name of God is also thus shown to be reasonably common throughout the Levant, in Moab as well as Egypt, and likely dating back to the times of Abraham and Joseph - those devout worshippers of this powerful God who hundreds of years earlier had also seen the impact and intervention of their God in affairs of state and the royal household, as well as publicly.

Throughout the region, from the time of Abraham, there could well have been pockets of adherents to this God, and Amenhotep may have boasted here about his seeming supremacy over all gods, including this one. Thus in temples like this one at Soleb he graphically portrayed them as conquered gods and peoples.

...proved that Amenhotep III had knowledge of this sacred Name of ... God.

Major evidence for the Exodus and an Amarna link:

The old gods were all discredited and publicly shamed at the same time.
The Egyptian army is uniquely missing during this period.
Horses are depicted only in a ceremonial, not military, role.
Soldiers are only depicted in ceremonial roles, or as foreign mercenaries.
Akhenaten, even if he trained a new army, seems fearful of fighting the Hebrews.
Egyptian gold is uniquely lacking during this period, just as Exodus explains.
A new emphasis on 'Truth' contrasts with the 'false' and dark religions and gods.
The huge religious change was unchallenged as a 'heresy' at the time.
The Aten now featured as the sole nameless truly powerful god rather than as an idol.
The Aten featured 'hands' at the end of each ray, reflecting recent divine experience.
Aten's change from falcon-headed to power-disk matches the timing of the Exodus.
'God' terminology suddenly destroys the need for a category of 'gods' ('neter').
Amenhotep III died suddenly, tragically, inexplicably, referred to as 'tragic death'.
Amenhotep III's mummy shows a violent death, being torn apart.
Amenhotep III's mummy was embalmed in a unique way with much resin.
Amenhotep III's mummy contains bird skeletons.
Amenhotep III's tomb is strangely unfinished and lacking proper status.
Amenhotep III's tomb contained a 'hub of a fine chariot'; likely related to his death.
Amenhotep III was a great builder, just as the Bible indicates.
Amenhotep III held strangely-timed frequent 'sed' feasts to raise the spirits of the people.
The Bible describes the Plagues, Pharoahs and Exodus in a way that matches this period.
Akhenaten was the second-born heir as Pharoah.
Akhenaten held a uniquely early 'sed' feast to raise the spirits of his bewildered people.
Amarna period 'was a reaction, not a planned revolution'; reaction to what?
Tiye wears royal crown demonstrating a temporary 'de facto' sole-ruler status.
Tiye addressed as though de-facto Queen while 2nd-born son still too young to rule.
Crown Prince Djhutmose died as firstborn heir, at a young age.
Crown Prince Djhutmose cause of death not evident.
Crown Prince Djhutmose buried with Tiye and close to father Amenhotep III.
Evidence for a co-regency between Amenhotep III and Akhenaten is lacking.
Ancient historians credit this period with the link to the Exodus.
Moses and other contemporary Hebrews were very likely to have influenced Akhenaten.
Other viziers and royal personnel are thought to have been Semitic.

Evidence for the Exodus:

The Passover has commemmorated these events for about 3500 years.
Christians also commemmorate the event's counterpart.

Secondary evidence for the Exodus and an Amarna link:

Amenhotep III's mummy contains pebbles.

Amenhotep III's mummy contains another man's big toe and arm parts.

Akhenaten overwhelmingly seen as a unique 'heretic', 'pacifist' or 'atheist' Pharoah.

Redford and others see the link of Moses and Amarna.

Egyptological chronology is notoriously unreliable and questioned.

There is no correspondence between Amenhotep III and Akhenaten.

Name changes from '-Amun' to '-Aten' for many people, in response to shaming of Amun.

Gold suddenly plentiful in Israelite hands; main source at the time would have been Egypt.

Amarna stelae (3 of them) say 'entire' army was 'expelled' with 'many of the people'.

Stela X omits any mention of the army coming to Amarna, in its list of leaders.

Amarna boundary stelae make no mention of army presence or defences.

Women have great predominance in Akhenaten's reign; shortage of male iconography.

No evidence can be sustained for a co-regency of Amenhotep III and IV.

The Aten (part of the cult of Ra) had a 'secret name' rather than a revealed name.

The Aten's tag ["itn"] literally means [divine] 'father'.

Many statues of Amenhotep III re-modelled as Rameses II; demonstrates low esteem.

Sudden mass departure of Semites from Waset (see Rosalie David's book).

Ben-ben symbol recalls likely origin of Egypt soon after massive Flood, as in Bible.

Ben-ben obelisk was one of Akhenaten's first projects; focus on 'true' origins.

Akhenaten startled people with common 'Late Egyptian' instead of classical language.

Royal chariot hub found in Amenhotep III tomb; fits his likely cause of death in Red Sea.

Most Amarna key personnel were 'new faces'; greatly reduced, missing, 'old' populace.

REFERENCES AND EXPLANATORY NOTES

Chapter 1 and Introduction:

1   (page 3) The name 'Amarna' is a much later invention. The original name of the new city was Akhet-Aten. The later name is loosely based on a local tribe and nearby village.

2   (page 10) See http://www.thehistoryblog.com/archives/29044 for discussion.

However, in March 2017 an alabaster statue of Queen Tiye was discovered, featuring the falcon head version of Aten, suggesting that she was a temporary ruler in Waset whilst Akhenaten was still quite young. See http://www.ancient-origins.net/news-history-archaeology/extremely-rare-alabaster-statue-queen-tiye-found-egyptian-funerary-temple-021300. Also see page 144 of this book for more detail and photograph.

2   (page 11) Including at least Letters ('EA'): 7, 9, 10, 11, 16, 20, 24, 26, 27, 29, 41, 91.

3   (page 12) Waset (meaning: 'Sceptre') was later renamed Thebes by the Greek writer Homer, and later still as Karnak by Arabic peoples, when Thebes had become a ruin. Luxor is the modern name for the active city there, whilst Thebes and Karnak are names used for the old sites nearby. It was Ahmose who had originally built Waset as a city and a district, with Amun as its god.

4   (page 17) http://www.archaeology.wiki/blog/2014/02/07/new-evidence-on-the-amenhotep-iii-and-amenhotep-iv-co-regency

5   (page 18) *American Journal of Physical Anthropology*, Vol 159, Supplement S61, January 2016, pages 216-231.

6   (page 19) *Recent Discoveries in Bible Lands,* p. 72, W F Albright, Biblical Colloquium.

7   (page 19) *The Seven Great Monarchies of the Ancient World*, vol. 1., chapter 3, para 13, by Prof Henry Rawlinson. Published by Alden, New York 1885. He adds in paragraph 2 that it *"conveys the exact truth... in accordance with the earliest classical traditions and with the latest results of modern comparative philology."*

8   (page 21) Scripture quotes generally taken from the *Tanakh* translation. Published by *The Jewish Translation Society,* 1985. Some quotes paraphrased with other translations.

9   (page 22) *The Royal Mummies*, by G Elliot Smith, pages 46-51. (Cairo, 1912)

10   (page 23) *http://mathstat.slu.edu/~bart/egyptianhtml/mummycaches/KV%2035.htm*

11   (page 27) Donald B. Redford, *Pharaonic King Lists, Annals and Day Books,* Benben Publications, 1986.

12 (page 28) *Egypt, Canaan, and Israel in Ancient Times,* Donald B. Redford, Princeton University Press, 1992, p. 377.

13 (page 30) *From Eden to Exile,* David Rohl (2009).

14 (page 30) *Patterns of Evidence: The Exodus* by Timothy P. Mahoney (film), 2016. Also http://www.patternsofevidence.com.

Chapter 2 (*The Amarna Letters*):

1   *The Amarna Letters*, William Moran, Johns Hopkins University Press, Baltimore, 1992.

2   (page 86) Libyan Mercenaries, depicted on British Museum papyrus fragments EA74100.

Chapter 3 (*The Exodus*):

1   (page 91) *YHWH,* commonly known as the Tetragrammaton ('4 letters'), and first used at Gen 2:4 [vowel-pointed later as *Yehowah*] where it would have been self-evident as to the underlying meaning of the Name. At Ex 3:14 it uses the powerful imperfect singular verb basis of the Name, as *'ehyeh - 'asher - 'ehyeh* or *"I will be that I will be"* (Isaac Leesers translation), or *"I will become whatsover I please"* (Rotherham's translation), thus amplifying His intention to take supernatural appropriate action whenever it was required, as specified here at Ex 3:20.   This meaning is hidden by the all-too-common rendering of the [imperfect tense verb] *'ehyeh* in English as *"I am"* instead of recognising its root *hayah* [*hyh* or interchanged sometimes with *hwh,* a Qal stem first-person singular imperfect verb; see excellent essay at drmsh.com/the-naked-bible/yhwh] (as in *havah nagila,* 'let us become... {happy}') and the underlying verb *'to redeem'* [Hebrew *hwy*] by action.   That verb *'ehyeh* is also discussed eloquently in Roy Zuck's 12-volume *Vital Old Testament Issues,* describing the verb as fully predicated (thus, not just *'I am'* but *'I will do'* assertively*)* and containing a *"phenomological view"* of issues. Simply stated, that God can, does and will take phenominal effective action in any way, in any circumstances, with unlimited power, as he evidently demonstrated in Egypt.

The *Qur'an,* according to the classical commentary *Tafsīr al-Jalālayn,* also speaks highly of 'Asaph, son of Berechiah. *'He was a righteous man. He knew God's greatest name, and whenever he called on it, he was answered.'* Interestingly, Psalm 83 in the *Bible* was written by this same Asaph and in verse 18 he specifies the actual name of God as YHWH. The popular tag *'Allah'* is equivalent to the relatively miscellaneous title *'The God'* in English, or *El-ohim* in Hebrew, which contains a plurality ('-im') of majesty.

2   (page 94) *Ipuwer Papyrus* (now in Leiden Museum, Netherlands). See *Ancient Egyptian Literature,* Volume I, p.150, by Miriam Lichtheim.

3   (page 94) *Egypt's Dazzling Sun: Amenhotep III and His World* , by Arielle Kozloff, Cambridge (1992)

4   (page 95) *Genesis of the Pharaohs: Dramatic New Discoveries That Rewrite the Origins of Ancient Egypt*, by Toby Wilkinson (2003)

Chapter 4 (The Shamed Exodus Pharoah):

1   (page 100) *Journal of the American Association of Physical Anthropologists*, Volume 159, Issue Supplement S61, January 2016, pp216–231.
See a summary also at: http://onlinelibrary.wiley.com/doi/10.1002/ajpa.22909/full

2   (page 101) *The Royal Mummies*. Cairo, Grafton Elliot Smith, (1912) with great mono photos by Brusch. See also a brief online summary at http://members.tripod.com/anubis4_2000/mummypages1/18B.htm#Amenhotep III

3   (page 101) It is possible that these breakages were caused by grave-robbers, yet the very extensive damage seems more likely to have been caused by other means.

4   (page 102) *Mysteries of the Mummies*, Dr Rosalie David, (1978)

5   (page 104) *X-Raying the Pharoahs* by Harris & Weeks (1973), also *An X-Ray Atlas of the Royal Mummies*, by Harris (1980).

6   (page 104) Aidan Dodson's *Amenhotep III: Uncles, Brothers, Sons, and the Serapeum.*

7   (page 105) WASEDA University site: *Interim report of the re-clearance at the royal tomb of Amenophis III (KV 22)* and   YOSHIMURA Sukuji, KONDO Jiro: *The tomb of Amenophis III: Waseda University expeditions 1989-2000*, Annales du Service des Antiquités de l'Égypte, 78, p. 205-209, Le Caire, 2004.

8   (page 105) Not to be confused with Crown Prince Djhutmose 'A' who had lived under a much earlier reign. Djhutmose is also spelled Thutmosis or Thutmose.   (Photo of cat sarcophagus; normally displayed in Cairo Museum)

9   (page 105) http://mathstat.slu.edu/~bart/egyptianhtml/mummycaches/KV%2035.htm

   The Valley of the Kings; the Decline of a Royal Necropolis , C. N. Reeves, (Keegan Paul Int, 1990) pp194, 198, 204-05, 210, 222-23 [n.129 & 168], 272;

   Egyptian Mummies, Grafton Elliot Smith & Warren Dawson, (Keegan Paul Int, 1991) pp93 and fig. 16.

   http://members.tripod.com/anubis4_2000/mummypages2/UnidentifiedandMissing.htm#Unidentified%20Boy

10 (page 107) http://www.archaeology.wiki/blog/2014/02/07/new-evidence-on-the-amenhotep-iii-and-amenhotep-iv-co-regency

Chapter 5 (The Effect of the Ten Plagues):

1   (page 112) Exodus 12:38

2   (page 112) *Pyramid Builders of Ancient Egypt: A Modern Investigation of Pharaohs Work-force* by Rosalie David, Routledge, 1986

3   (page 112) *Akhenaten-the Heretic King*, Don Redford.

4   (page 113) Meskell, L. 2002. *Private Life in New Kingdom Egypt.* Oxford: Princeton University Press.   Also the illustrated essay by Emmelia Booth; https://www.academia.edu/7184794/*The_Interaction_Between_the_Living_and_the_Dead_at_Deir_el-Medina*

5   (page 113) (Photograph on page) Limestone stele of a woman kneeling before two ancestor busts. Provenance: Deir el-Medina Source: British Museum [online] http://www.britishmuseum.org/research/collection_online/collection_object_details.aspx?objectId=120842&partId=1&object=20160&sortBy =imageName&page=1

6   (page 114) *Book of Enoch* (an apocyphal book, not actually written by Enoch, but the product of an unknown author around 100 - 300 BCE.

7   (page 115) Babel; see Genesis 10 and 11.

8   (page 115) *Mythologies*, Yves Bonnefoy; 2 volumes. University of Chicago Press, 1991

9   (page 116) *Antiquities of the Jews*, 2.10.1 , Josephus.

10   (page 117) *Mythologies* p123-4, 'Serapis', was absorbed into the Greek, then the Roman trinity with Isis and Horus, as a replacement for the original Egyptian Osiris in the 'godhead'.

11   (page 117) *Texts from the Amarna Period in Egypt*, p73. Murnane.

12   (page 117) *Amenhotep III; Perspectives on his Reign*, J Baines, 2004,-p.287

13   (page 117) *Egyptian Solar Religion in the New Kingdom; Re, Amun and the Crisis of Polytheism,* Assmann (1995,-p.158) London. Kegan Paul International.

14   (page 117) *Religion of the living in Ancient Egypt*, Anth. 446 Ppt. Lecture 6: by Mumford; 2014 Anth.446/646) (PDF with many pics; tacky but concisely explained).

16   (page 121) *The Complete Temples of Ancient Egypt*, Wilkinson, 2000 p.164

17   (page 121) *The Oxford Encyclopaedia of Ancient Egypt*, Volume 1, Schlogl, 2001 p.156

18   (page 122) *Akhenaten-the Heretic King*, Don Redford, p73-76

19   (page 123) *Texts from the Amarna Period in Egypt*, p30. Murnane, 1995. Scholars Press.

20   (page 123) *Texts from the Amarna Period in Egypt*, p213-242. Murnane.

21   (page 124) http://www.maat.sofiatopia.org/aten.htm (good essay on the whole topic)

22   (page 125) Lichtheim, M. : *Ancient Egyptian Literature*, University of California Pres
          California, 1976, vol.II, pp.96-100.

     Translated again here by: http://www.sacred-texts.com/egy/rtae/rtae13.htm
     Internet Sacred Text Archive (ISTA)   Santa Cruz, CA 95061-7429 USA

23   (page 125) British Museum Stela, No. 826. It is accessible only in two very incorrect
     copies, published by Birch, Trans. Soc. Bib. Arch., VIII, 143, and Pierret, in his Recueil, I.

24   (page 127) *Akhenaten-the Heretic King*, Don Redford, p176.

25   Ibid page 208, translated and quoted from Urk IV 2027ff - *Urkunden des Agypttischen
     Altertums*. Leipzig 1903.

26   (page 127) *Religion and Magic in Ancient Egypt,* Rosalie David, Routledge. 2002. p.218

27   (page 127) *Texts from the Amarna Period in Egypt*, p77. Murnane.

28   (page 127) *The Oxford Encyclopaedia of Ancient Egypt*, Volume 1 Quirke. 2001,-p.12/16

29   (page 127) Ibid Vol 1 Schlogl. p.156

30   (page 128) Ibid Vol 1 Eaton-Krauss p.49

31   (page 128) *Religion and Magic in Ancient Egypt,* Rosalie David. 2002 p.218.

32   (page 129) *Akhenaten-the Heretic King*, Don Redford, p130.

33   (page 129) Ibid, p131.

34   (page 131) *Patterns of Evidence: The Exodus* by Timothy P. Mahoney (film), 2016.

Chapter 6 (A New World at Amarna):

1   (page 138) *News from Nowhere,* William Morris.

2   (page 138) *Akhenaten-the Heretic King*, Don Redford, p149.

3   (page 138) *The Rock Tombs of El-Amarna*, 6 volumes; by N de G Davies.

4-5 (page 143-4) See several publications by *Zivie and Gessler-Lohr* on excavations at Saqqara.

6   (page 146) *The Essence of Amarna Monotheism,* Goldwasser, Orly. 2006.
     Seminar für Ägyptologie und Koptologie: Göttingen.

7   (page 147) *Akhenaten: King of Egypt,* Cyril Aldred, 1988, 1991. Thames & Hudson.

8   (page 147) *Ancient Egypt ,* Barry Kemp. p70.

9   (page 147) *Ancient Egyptian Readings,* Wim van den Dungen.

Chapter 7 (Other Inscriptions):

1   (page 154) *"The Amarna Boundary Stelae"* by John Johnson (Horus Egyptology Society),
     p113 (with detailed interlinear on page 76) available directly from farrimondjohnson@
     talk21.com and in support of the 'Colossi of Memnon' Project.

2   (page 157) *Antiquities of the Jews,* Whiston, English translation; 2.9.2 footnote.

     also *Against Apion*, Josephus 1.26.

3   (page 159) *Pharaonic King-Lists,* Don Redford, p. 293.

4   (page 159) *Geography,* Strabo, lib. xvi., c.2.

5   (page 161) Michela Schiff Giorgini et Clément Robichon, *Soleb II, les nécropoles*, Sansoni,
     Florence, 1971.

6   (page 161) 'Finkelstein; https://www.biblearchaeology.org/post/2010/02/04/Amenho-
     tep-II-and-the-Historicity-of-the-Exodus-Pharaoh.aspx#Article
     (See comments following that article, also)

7   (page 157) *Divinity of Doubt: the God Question,* Bugliosi·

Why Faith Matters, Rabbi Wolpe (http://www.beliefnet.com/faiths/judaism/2004/12/ did-the-exodus-really-happen.aspx?p=2)

See also Norma Franklin (*The Zinman Institute of Archaeology* University of Haifa),

8   (page 162) *Pharaoh's People - Scenes from Life in Imperial Egypt,* T.G.H. James, former Keeper in Department of Egyptian Antiquities at British Museum, 1984. Bodley Head.

9   (page 163) Rohl; *New Chronology,* various works.

10   (page 163) 'See http://kgov.com/exodus-patterns-of-evidence-from-ancient-egypt-timothy-mahoney-interview

Patterns of Evidence: The Exodus by Timothy P. Mahoney (film), 2016.

Chapter 8 (The Hapiru):

1   (page 166) See detailed discussion of inscriptions at: https://www.revolvy.com/main/index.php?s=Habiru

2   (page 166) L B Paton, *Journal of Biblical Literature,* XXXII [1913] pp38
Israel's Conquest of Canaan.

3   (page 166) W F Albright (1943 paper, p29)

4   (page 167) *Bitter Lives: Israel in and out of Egypt.* Carol Redmount.

5   (page 167) Pfeiffer (1963, 53).

6   **(pic)** One of the Abu Simbal Photos of the 1905 Breasted Expedition to Egypt first published by the oriental Institute.

BIBLIOGRAPHY:

Albright W F; "*The Amarna Letters from Palestine*" Cambridge Ancient History, 1966.

Albright W F; *"Recent Discoveries in Bible Lands"*, p. 72, Biblical Colloquium.

Aldred, C : *"Akhenaten, King of Egypt"*, Thames and Hudson - London, 1988.

Assmann, J: *"Moses the Egyptian"*, Harvard University - London, 1997.

Assmann, J: *"The Search for God in Ancient Egypt"*, Cornell University Press - 2001.

Assmann, J: *"Egyptian Solar Religion in the New Kingdom; Re, Amun and the Crisis of Polytheism"*, London. Kegan Paul International.

Astour, Michael C; *"Habiru."* Interpreter's Dictionary of the Bible, Supplementary Volume, Keith Crim (editor), Nashville: Abingdon, 1976.

Atlantisonline: *"The Amarna Letters".* http://atlantisonline.smfforfree2.com/index.php?topic=14244.0

Baines, J; "*Amenhotep III; Perspectives on his Reign*", 2004.

Bierbrier, M L; *"The British Museum: Heiroglyphic Texts from Egyptian Stelae"*, Vol 10, British Museum (1982).

Blaikie, James FRAS; *"The Amarna Age; a study of the crisis of the ancient world"*; published by A&C Black, London. [some out of date information, inaccurate map, agrees that Hapiru not the Hebrews]; 1926.

Bonnefoy; "Mythologies" (2 volumes). University of Chicago Press, 1991.

Booth, Charlotte; *"Lost Voices of the Nile",* Amberley Publishing, 2015.

Breasted, J H: *"Ancient Records of Egypt"*, University of Illinois Press - 2001.

Breasted, J H: *"Development of Religion and Thought in Ancient Egypt"*, Pennsylvania Press - Pennsylvania, 1972.

Breasted, J H : *"On the Hymns to the Sun composed under Amenophis IV"*, Berlin University - (dissertation), 1895.

Budge, E A W : *"The Gods of the Egyptian"*, Dover - New York, 1969, vol.1.

Campbell, Edward A; *"The Amarna Letters and the Amarna Period."* Biblical Archaeologist Reader, Vol. 3, pp54-75. New York. Doubleday, 1970.

Chaney, Marvin L; *"Ancient Palestinian Peasant Movements and the Formation of Premonarchic Israel."* Social World of Biblical Antiquity Series 2. Sheffield. Almond, 1983.

David, Rosalie; *"Mysteries of the Mummies", 1979.*

David, Rosalie; *"Pyramid Builders of Ancient Egypt: A Modern Investigation of Pharaohs Workforces", ,* Routledge, 1986

Davies, N de G: *"Rock Tombs of El Amarna, Archaeological Survey of Egypt"*- London, 1908.

Dodson, Aidan; "*Amenhotep III: Uncles, Brothers, Sons, and the Serapeum".*

Hull, Edward, 1890; *Deacon's Synchronological Chart of Universal History.* Studio Editions.

Drury, Allen; *"A God against the Gods",* Doubleday (1976)

Edersheim, Alfred; *Old Testament Bible History.*

El-Daly, Okasha; *"Egyptology: The Missing Millenium: Ancient Egypt in Medieval Arabic Writings",* UCL Press, (2005).

Fletcher, Joann; *"Egypt's Sun King",* 2000.

Garstang, John; *"The Foundations of Bible History".* 1931.

Gertoux G; *"Moses and the Exodus - Chronological, Historical & Archaeological Evidence",* 2015.

Ginsberg, Louis; *"Legends of the Jews"* . 1925.

Gohary, J; *"Akhenaten's Sed-Festival at Karnak",* Kegan Paul Int, 1992.

Goldwasser, Orly; *"The Origins of the Alphabet",* Cambridge Scholars, 2015.

Goldwasser, Orly; *"The Essence of Amarna Monotheism".*

Gonen, Rivka; *"Urban Canaan in Late Bronze Age."* Bulletin of the American Schools of Oriental Research 253. 1981.

Hallock, F H; *"The Habiru and the SA.GAZ in the Tell El-Amarna Tablets."* Mercer 1939.

Harris & Weeks; *"X-Raying the Pharoahs"* 1973, also *An X-Ray Atlas of the Royal Mummies,* by Harris 1980.

Hart, G: *"A Dictionary of Egyptian Gods & Goddesses",* Routledge & Kegan - London, 1986.

Hawass; *"Scanning the Pharoahs",* 2015.

Hornung, E. : *"Akhenaten and the Religion of Light",* Cornell University Press - 1999.

Hornung, E: *"The Ancient Egyptian Books of the Afterlife",* Cornell University Press - Ithaca.

IBSA; 1988. *Insight on the Scriptures*

James, T G H (British Museum); 2007; *Pharaoh's People: Scenes from Life in Imperial Egypt*

Johnson, John; *"Amarna Stelae",* Wigan Egyptology Society. 2016.

Johnson, W Raymond; *"Amenhotep III and Amarna: Some New Considerations.",* Egypt Exploration Society, 1996

Josephus, F; "*Antiquities of the Jews" (translation by Whiston).*

Journal of The American Association of Physical Anthropologists. Jan 2016

Kozloff & Bryan,: *"Egypt's Dazzling Sun : Amenhotep III and His World",* Cleveland, 1992.

Lemche, Niels Peter; *"Habiru / Hapiru."* Anchor Bible Dictionary, edited by David Noel Freedman, 3:6-10. New York: Doubleday, 1992.

Lichtheim, M: *"Ancient Egyptian Literature",* California University Press - vol 1, 1975.

Mahoney, T P; *"Patterns of Evidence: The Exodus".* (film) 2016.

Mercer; *"Tutankhamen and Egyptology".* 1923.

Meskell, L; *Private Life in New Kingdom Egypt.* 2002.

Metropolitan Museum Bulletin 17 . 1922; *"The Pharoah of the Exodus".*

Mitchell, T C; *"The Bible in the British Museum"*, British Museum Press, 1988.

Moran, William: *"The Amarna Letters"*, Johns Hopkins Univ. Press - Baltimore, 1992.

Moseley; *"Amarna; the missing evidence"*, 2009.

Murane, W J: *"Ancient Egyptian Coregencies"*, Studies in Ancient Oriental Civilization, Chicago, No.40, 1977, pp.123-169.

Murane, W J: *"On the Accession date of Akhenaten"*, Studies in Honor of George R Hughes, The Oriental Institute - Chicago, 1977, pp.163-167.

Murnane, William J; *"Texts from the Amarna Period in Egypt"*, Scholars Press, Atlanta, Georgia.

Oriental Institute of Chicago (Touring exhibition organised by Museum of Fine Arts, Boston, with artefacts from Cairo); *"Pharoahs of the Sun." (commemmorative catalogue), 2000.*

Pfeiffer, Charles F; *"Tell El Amarna and the Bible"*, Baker Studies in Biblical Archaelogy, 1963.

Quirke, Stephen; *"The Cult of Ra"*, 2001. Thames & Hudson.

Rawlinson, Henry; *The Seven Great Monarchies of the Ancient World*, Alden, New York 1885.

Redford, Donald B; *"Akhenaten, the Heretic King"*, Princeton, 1984.

Redford, Donald B; *"Egypt, Canaan, and Israel in Ancient Times,"*, Princeton, 1992.

Redford, Donald B; *"Pharaonic King Lists, Annals and Day Books"*.

Rohl, D; "From Eden to Exile". 2009.

Schlogl; "*The Oxford Encyclopaedia of Ancient Egypt*", Volume 1. 2001.

Sattin, Anthony; *"The Pharoah's Shadow"*, 2000.

Smith, Elliott, *"The Royal Mummies"*; 1905.

Spencer A Jeffrey (Author). *"The British Museum Book of Ancient Egypt* – 2007.

Van den Dungen; "*Ancient Egyptian Readings*"

Velikovsky; *"Ages in Chaos"*, 1952.

Watterson, Barbara; *"Amarna, Ancient Egypt's Age of Revolution"*. Family tree with cartouches.

Weigall, A. : *"The Life and Times of Akhenaten"*, Pharaoh of Egypt, Edinburgh, 1910.

Wikimedia resource: *"Localities and their Rulers"*. https://en.wikipedia.org/wiki/Amarna_letters%E2%80%93localities_and_their rulers

Wilkinson, J G. : *"Manners and Customs of the Ancient Egyptians"*, London, 1837.

Wilkinson, J G; "*The Complete Temples of Ancient Egypt*". 2000.

Wilkinson, Toby; "*Genesis of the Pharaohs: Dramatic New Discoveries That Rewrite the Origins of Ancient Egypt*" 2003

Winckler, Hugo. *"The Tell-el-Amarna Letters"*. Translated by J. Metcalf. New York: Lemcke & Buechner, 1896.

PERMISSIONS AND PICTURE ATTRIBUTION:

Page

1   Montage from Creative Commons BY SA and author's museum photos.

         Cartouche drawn by author; CC BY SA

         Device drawn by author. CC BY SA

3   CC BY SA 2.5 wikipedia.com

4   CC BY SA 2.0 wikipedia.com (both images)

5   Main photo by Smith, 1905. Inset photo by Victor Loret, 1898.

         Artefact is in chamber Jc, KV 35. Public domain.

         Amenhotep III mummy'. Creative Commons BY SA 2.0

6   Montage adaptation by author. Some are from Ziad Nour, authorised for this author as 'public domain' on Feb 3rd 2017.

7   Creative Commons 2.0 by Les Williams, at Seattle exhibition.

8   From *The Royal Mummies*. Cairo, Smith Grafton Elliot, (1912) with great mono photos by Brusch. Public domain.

11   CC BY SA 2.5 wikipedia.com

13   Diana Haret, 2017, by courtesy of Berlin museum.

14   © Adobe Stock; licenced image 45959626

20   CC-BY-SA Source: The Fitzwilliam Museum, Camridge, UK http://data.fitzmuseum.com.ac.uk/id/object/58984

21   Author's photo, by courtesy of Israel Museum, Jerusalem. CC BY SA

         Tomb: CC BY SA 2.0 wikipedia.com

22   Author's photo, by courtesy of British Museum. CC BY SA

23   Brusch, 1912. Public domain.

24   Brusch, 1912. Public domain.

26   Author's photo, by courtesy of Met Art Museum.

30   Author's photo, by courtesy of Met Art Museum.

31   Drawn by author. CC BY SA

32   Montage by author, from public domain sources. Mount clips and shadows added.

38   © Adobe Stock; licenced image 21689167

47   CC BY SA 2.0

49   CC BY SA 2.0

53   Author's photo.

57   CC BY SA 2.0

85   Public domain.

89   Author's photo. CC BY SA

95   Public domain.

96-97   © Catmando. Extended Licence from Fotolia.

96   Inset 1: Author's photo, courtesy of Met Art museum.

         Inset 2: see page 103

98	Public domain.
99	Public domain.
100-2	From *The Royal Mummies*. Cairo, Smith Grafton Elliot, (1912) with great mono photos by Brusch. Public domain.
102	Drawn by author.
104	Public domain.
106	Author's and tour guide photos, by courtesy of The Louvre, Paris.
107	Tour guide photo, by courtesy of New Museum, Berlin.
108	Drawn by author, based on 'The Cult of Ra' by Stephen Quirke.
110	Tour guide photo, by courtesy of New Museum, Berlin.
110-111	© Leonid Andronov. Extended Licence from Fotolia.
112	CC BY SA 2.0
113	Tour guide photo, by courtesy of British Museum.
114-6	Public domain.
117	CC BY SA 2.0 Courtesy of National Museums Scotland.
118	From: *Texts from the Amarna Period in Egypt* Murnane. © Adobe Stock; licenced image 143048763 Baal: Author's photo, by courtesy of Israel Museum, Jerusalem.
119	From *The Royal Mummies*. Cairo, Smith Grafton Elliot, (1912) with great mono photos by Brusch. Public domain.
120	Public domain.
121	Tour guide photo, by courtesy of New Museum, Berlin.
122	Public domain. Luxor museum.
124	Public domain.
128	Public domain.
133	CC BY SA 2.0
134	Amarna: Public domain. Relief: Author's photo, courtesy of Met Art museum. Lips: Author's photo, courtesy of Met Art museum.
136	Creative Commons 2.0 by Les Williams, at Seattle exhibition.
137	© Adobe Stock; licenced image 92335475
138	CC BY SA 2.0
139	Author's photo and clipped, courtesy of Met Art museum.
140	CC BY SA 2.0 CC BY SA 2.0
144	Public domain. Courtesy of Egyptian Ministry of Antiquities.
145	From *The Royal Mummies*. Cairo, Smith Grafton Elliot, (1912) with great mono photos by Brusch. Public domain.
151	CC BY SA 2.0
152	© Paul Docherty, with permission. www.pauldocherty.com © John Johnson, donated.

155   Drawn by author, based on S Waite & D Hitchen in John Johnson book.

156   Drawn by author. CC BY SA

160   CC BY SA 2.0

164   Matthew Harris, courtesy of British Museum.

167   CC BY SA 2.0

168   CC BY SA 2.0

ACKNOWLEDGEMENTS:

Anne Jackson ('Anne of the Nile'), for initial reading & encouragement to publish.

John Johnson (Wigan Egyptology Society), for detail on Waset and Gebil El Silsila.

Russ Holden (Pixeltweaks), for early ebook and publishing assistance.

Derek House & Associates, for typesetting.

British Museum, for the display of some Amarna Letters, and support.

Paul Teague, for professional author guidance.

EGYPTIAN WORDS, PREFIXES:

Akhen	beneficial
Akhet	inundation, horizon
Khty	horizon
Hotep	content
Khepr	eternal life
Thut	Thoth
Mosis	born
Men	manifest
Re	ra, [primary sun god]
Nefer	beauty
Neb	lord
Nefer	good, beautiful
Uraei	snake, symbol of sovereignty

INTERCHANGEABLE SPELLINGS, WORDS AND TITLES

Abram	Abraham (later name in Canaan and Egypt)
Akhenaten	Akenaton, Ikhanaton, Naphurure-ya, Amenhotep IV (before his 5th year of reign), Akhenamun, Amenophis IV
Amarna	Akhet-Aten ('The Horizon of the Aten')
Amenhotep III	Nimmureya, Nibmuareya, Neb-Maat-Re, Amenophis III (Greek)
Amun	Amen
Apiru	Habiru, Hapiru
Aten	Aton
Babylon	Sumerians (from Sumer region; non-Semitic)
BCE	BC, Before Common Era (more accurate term)
Bible	*Torah*, Hebrew Scriptures, Christian Greek Scriptures, Pentateuch, 'Hebrew *Bible*'
Byblos	Gubla, Gubal, Geval, Jbail (Arabic), Gebal, Geval
Djhutmose	Thutmose, Tutmose (A & B), Thutmosis
Gem-pa-Aten	['The Aten is Found'], 'Long Temple' (term used by *Amarna Project*), [Akhenaten's temple built in first 5 reign years]
Hebrews	Semites [from Shem], Israelites [nation formed while in Egypt, belong to Israel/Jacob], Jews [specifically belong to Judah, but became a generic term for all Israelites]
Heliopolis	On, 'sun city'
KV	WV (for the West Valley tombs; same numbering sequence). 'King's Valley' and 'West Valley' respectively
Pharoah	King ('Pharoah' originally referred to the house of the ruler, but later became the term for the ruler himself)
Re	Ra
Qur'an	Koran
YHWH	Yahweh, Jehovah, Yehowah [God, Creator, The God, El-ohim]
Waset	Thebes (Greek), No Amun (in *Nahum*), No (in *Ezekiel*), Luxor, [includes the temple area of Karnak]

Index of key words

.

Printed in Great Britain
by Amazon